Twentieth Century
Painting and Sculpture
in the Philadelphia
Museum of Art

Twentieth Century Painting and Sculpture in the Philadelphia Museum of Art

Ann Temkin

Susan Rosenberg

Michael Taylor

and contributions by Rachael Arauz

Philadelphia Museum of Art

Copyright 2000 Philadelphia Museum of Art

Produced by the Department of Publishing
Philadelphia Museum of Art
Benjamin Franklin Parkway at Twenty-Sixth Street
P.O. Box 7646
Philadelphia, PA 19101-7646

Edited by Jane Watkins
Production by Richard Bonk

Designed by Tsang Seymour Design, Inc., New York
Color separations by Professional Graphics, Inc., Rockford, Illinois
Printed and bound by Arnoldo Mondadori Editore, S.p.A., Verona, Italy

Photographs are by Graydon Wood, Lynn Rosenthal, and Eric Mitchell,
Photography Department, Philadelphia Museum of Art

Library of Congress Cataloging-in-Publication Data

Philadelphia Museum of Art.
       Twentieth Century painting and sculpture in the Philadelphia Museum of Art

       Ann Temkin, Susan Rosenberg, and Michael Taylor, with Rachael Arauz.
       p. cm.
   Includes bibliographical references and index.
   ISBN 0-87633-133-9 – ISBN 0-87633-132-0 (pbk.)
    1. Art, Modern–20th century–Catalogs.
      2. Art–Pennsylvania–Philadelphia–Catalogs.
      3. Philadelphia Museum of Art–Catalogs. I. Temkin, Ann. II. Rosenberg,
      Susan, 1963– III. Taylor, Michael, 1966– IV. Title.

                  N6487.P45 P486 2000
                  709'.04'007474811–dc21
                      00-038502

ISBN 0-87633-132-0 (paper)
ISBN 0-87633-133-9 (cloth)

Printed and bound in Italy

NEUBERGER BERMAN

This publication is supported by a generous grant from the Neuberger Berman,
LLC Fund at The New York Community Trust.

Preface

At the turn of the twenty-first century, as the Philadelphia Museum of Art prepares to celebrate its 125th anniversary in 2001, what could be more appropriate than to publish a book surveying the Museum's remarkable collections of twentieth-century painting and sculpture. The institution's commitment to the visual arts of its own time goes back to its founding in 1876 and to the Centennial Exposition, from which examples of the latest styles in the decorative arts were acquired. The Museum's first acquisition fund for paintings, the W. P. Wilstach Fund, received in 1893, was spent a few years later on a major painting by the then contemporary artist Henry O. Tanner. In the first half of the twentieth century, the Museum had all too little in the way of purchase monies and a long way to go to fill several acres of galleries with the art of many centuries and several continents; spectacular purchases were made, such as Cézanne's *Large Bathers* in 1937, but its great holdings of the work of modern artists came primarily as the gifts of inspired collectors. If there is a single spirit presiding over the modern and contemporary galleries, it is that of Marcel Duchamp. Rigorously anti "art with a capital A" with regard to his own work, Duchamp had a keen and sympathetic eye for the art of his contemporaries, and it was through his aegis that splendid works by Brancusi, Miró, and Mondrian, to name only a few, were acquired by his friends Louise and Walter Arensberg. The Arensbergs were also intent on assembling a matchless collection of Duchamp's own work. When they asked for his help in determining the best home for their collection, and he found a suite of Philadelphia's then empty galleries much to his liking, the die was cast for this Museum's future as a magnet for new art.

The presence of Duchamp's *Large Glass* on the cover of this book reminds us that it remains, more than 75 years after being "definitively unfinished," perhaps the most influential work in all of twentieth-century art (with the possible exception of several innocent-looking Readymades that share the same gallery). Standing where Duchamp installed it in 1954, his *Glass* has reflected the faces of generations of puzzled visitors, devoted scholars, and young artists from around the world who gaze at and through its transparent surface into new dimensions of invention.

Knowing from my own happy experience what a thrill it was when I was a young curator working with this collection, it is a delight to see the same thrill pervade the admirable team headed by Ann Temkin, who have not only written elegantly and concisely about the objects in this book, but continue to shape and build the collection in new directions at once thoughtful and exciting. Choosing from more than fifteen hundred works was an impossible task, with many favorites omitted of necessity, yet we hope that the selection tempts both reader and viewer to come back for more.

George Marcus has produced another fine example of the books he works so hard to make informative and appealing introductions to the Museum's collections; Jane Watkins's thoughtful editing unifies an inevitably disparate mix of objects and texts as does Patrick Seymour's handsome design.

For the financial support to make such a handsome publication possible, we are enormously grateful to Neuberger Berman, LLC Fund at The New York Community Trust.

We put this book into your hands to draw you further into the Museum, into its great collections, and into the extraordinary, unexpected, unfolding world of the art of our own time.

Anne d'Harnoncourt
The George D. Widener Director and Chief Executive Officer

The Origins of the Collection

The art of the twentieth century stands among the great glories of the Philadelphia Museum of Art. From the vantage point of the year 2000, much of this collection is regarded as classic, and even the art that still appears experimental or provocative seems rightfully at home in a public museum. In the early part of the twentieth century, however, the purchase or display of avant-garde paintings and sculpture depended far less on American museums than on a few courageous and astute private individuals. These collectors' residences or galleries (almost as much as the studios of the artists themselves) served as laboratories in which the art of their time was nurtured and explored. The collection of twentieth-century art at the Philadelphia Museum of Art came into being as an aggregate of the accomplishments of such early pioneers. Its great distinction—and superbly good fortune—is the degree to which it is shaped by gifts not only of individual works of art but also of entire collections with their own strong personalities. The resulting holdings of the Museum are furthermore remarkable for the extent to which those original collections were formed in close collaboration with artists themselves. No better experts could be found.

The first gift that gave the Philadelphia Museum of Art a true collection of contemporary art was that of Albert Eugene Gallatin. It was, in a sense, the gift of a museum to a museum. A lifelong New Yorker born in 1881 in Villanova, Pennsylvania, Gallatin was a patrician by birth, a lawyer by training, and an art collector by preference. In 1927, spurred on by the indifference that public institutions displayed toward the art of their own time, he established this country's first museum of modern art with a permanent collection. He called it the Gallery of Living Art—later he changed the name to the Museum of Living Art—and housed it at New York University, where he was a trustee. Gallatin liked to emphasize the experimental nature of his venture by pointing out that the gallery was located on the site of the building on Washington Square in which Samuel F. B. Morse, while professor at New York University's art department, invented the magnetic telegraph.

Gallatin himself became a painter and a founding member of the group called the American Abstract Artists, although he modestly admitted that he painted only to better understand the pictures he collected. As reflected in his own work, Gallatin's taste was austere; he preferred geometric abstraction to figurative or expressionist imagery. His collecting activity relied heavily upon the warm friendships he developed over the years with fellow artists who served as avant-garde tutors and guides to Paris, where he spent part of every year. His sojourns are documented in photographic portraits Gallatin made of artists in their studios; he posed them in his own image, looking like elegant gentlemen rather than bohemians. He often purchased paintings directly from the artists, such as Fernand Léger's *The City*, which he bought after spying it rolled up in a corner of the painter's studio. When the Museum of Modern Art was established in uptown New York in 1929, Gallatin relished the often fierce competition for important acquisitions from Picasso and other artists.

A. E. Gallatin
(American, 1881–1952)
Untitled No. 106, 1949
Oil on canvas, 20 x 24 inches
Philadelphia Museum of Art. Gift of Mrs. Virginia M. Zabriskie

Piet Mondrian in his studio, 1934, photographed by A. E. Gallatin
(Philadelphia Museum of Art. A. E. Gallatin Archives)

Installation view of the Museum of Living Art at New York University in 1938 with Fernand Léger's *The City*
(Philadelphia Museum of Art. A. E. Gallatin Archives)

The Museum of Living Art thrived in Washington Square despite its undistinguished accommodations in a ground-floor space used as a study area. Provisional walls were fitted between free-standing fluted columns to provide room for changing installations of Gallatin's ever-growing collection. The Museum was open free each weekday from 8:00 a.m. until 10:00 p.m. and Saturdays as well. Oblivious students may have studied within its walls, but, at the same time, established or aspiring artists ranging from Arshile Gorky to Philip Guston were nourished on the works of art they encountered there.

In December 1942, New York University abruptly informed Gallatin that the collection could no longer be accommodated given the need for wartime economies. The enterprising director of the Philadelphia Museum of Art at the time, Fiske Kimball, read a story to this effect in *The New York Times* and immediately contacted Gallatin to ask if he would consider Philadelphia as the collection's next home. By the end of January 1943 the two had signed an agreement for an immediate loan and ultimate bequest of more than 160 works of art. The opening of the inaugural display in May attracted Philadelphia's art community as well as distinguished visitors from New York including Marcel Duchamp and Fernand Léger.

Gallatin's gift to the Museum was followed by that of Louise and Walter Arensberg, whose collection constitutes the other cornerstone of twentieth-century art in Philadelphia. The Arensbergs moved from Cambridge, Massachusetts, to New York in 1914, having decided to head for the epicenter of the art world shortly after seeing the Armory Show. Settling into an apartment on the Upper West Side, they immediately began buying art with guidance from a few artist and dealer friends. A year later they were fortunate enough to meet Marcel Duchamp shortly after his arrival from Paris. Although he was a newcomer to New York, Duchamp was already famous for his *Nude*

Louise and Walter Arensberg's apartment,
33 West 67th Street, New York City, about
1918, photographed by Charles Sheeler
(Philadephia Museum of Art. Arensberg Archives)

Descending a Staircase, the *succès de scandale* of the Armory Show. The Arensbergs
offered Duchamp the apartment above them, where he was free to concentrate on his
Readymades and the fabrication of *The Bride Stripped Bare by Her Bachelors, Even
(The Large Glass)*. Walter Arensberg became a close friend and collaborator of
Duchamp as well as a patron.

The Arensbergs' high-ceiling apartment was rapidly filled with European and American
art of the current moment. Matisse's *Mademoiselle Yvonne Landsberg* hung over the
fireplace near paintings by Duchamp, Francis Picabia, and Georges Braque. The
Arensbergs' enthusiasm, like that of many modern artists and art aficionados, extended
beyond Western cultures, and their superb African sculptures were interspersed with
contemporary works of art. The apartment functioned as a museum in the sense that
the Arensbergs were rarely alone: a cross section of the city's literary and artistic
avant-garde filled their rooms for frequent, lively open-house evenings.

In the 1920s the Arensbergs moved to Hollywood, and began the second phase of
their collecting life. Duchamp was back in Paris, but during the coming years he
assiduously served as a long-distance art consultant. He offered them not only his
own work but that of friends and peers, most notably a wealth of outstanding sculptures by Constantin Brancusi. Duchamp's advice reflects a remarkably catholic taste:
in one year he commended to his friends a new work by Marc Chagall and another
by Piet Mondrian. The Arensbergs' capacious house, furnished with beautiful antique

carpets and furniture, and graced with a modernist addition by California architect Richard Neutra, had no empty space. The African and modern art was joined by the pre-Columbian sculpture they bought voraciously in California and displayed both indoors and out.

Meanwhile, *The Large Glass* had been given a new home back East, since the Arensbergs decided against the risk of its cross-country transport. They sold it to Katherine Dreier, an artist and collector who in 1920 had established an organization named the Société Anonyme, with Duchamp and Man Ray as co-founders. Even earlier than A. E. Gallatin, Dreier had recognized the American public's need to see vanguard art, including that of artists from Eastern Europe and South America. The Société Anonyme organized intermittent but influential exhibitions and publications of international art in various venues in New York City. Dreier kept her own large collection in The Haven, her house in West Redding, Connecticut, where *The Large Glass* stood under the slanting wooden eaves of a commodious library. Whatever the ultimate disposition of her collection was to be, it was stipulated that *The Large Glass* would rejoin the Arensberg holdings.

By the end of the 1940s, when the Arensbergs began to ponder an ultimate home for their collection, the works they had collected were widely recognized as treasures. Several museums specifically devoted to contemporary art had been established by

Louise and Walter Arensberg's house in Hollywood, California, about 1948, photographed by Floyd Faxon (Philadelphia Museum of Art. Arensberg Archives)

then, and even encyclopedic museums recognized their oversight in ignoring the work
of their own era. After the Arensbergs dissolved a previous agreement with the Los
Angeles County Museum of Art, museum directors and trustees across the country
sought to win their collection. On the advice of his new ally A. E. Gallatin, Fiske Kimball
joined in the fray. Kimball emphasized the Museum's still-unfinished northeast wing,
which provided ready and ample ground for the Arensbergs' modern art as well as
their pre-Columbian objects. Based largely on good chemistry not only between the
two men but also their wives, the Arensbergs began to weigh Philadelphia's overtures
seriously. Their positive feelings were reinforced when Duchamp, who was sent to
Philadelphia in 1949 as a secret scout, reported to them his pleasure with the
Museum building's "feeling of permanence."

A gift was formalized the following year, and construction of the new wing began in
earnest. Sadly, neither Arensberg lived to see their collection in its new home: Louise
died in 1953 and Walter a few months later in 1954 (Gallatin had died in 1952, Dreier
also in 1953). But Duchamp remained in close contact with the Museum as plans for
the galleries developed. He personally supervised the installation of *The Large Glass* in
the position it still occupies, facing the East Terrace fountain through a tall window.
Extensive preparations culminated in the grand openings of the Gallatin and Arensberg
collections in the spring and fall of 1954, respectively. Duchamp, his wife, and friends
took the train from New York for the festive occasion. As fate would have it, a hurri-
cane disrupted their journey, and the group arrived at the Museum, dressed in black
tie, only the following morning.

At this time, Philadelphia's collection of twentieth-century art was developing on other fronts. Alfred Stieglitz, legendary champion of modern art in the United States, was another generous benefactor of the Museum, through the agency of his widow Georgia O'Keeffe. Stieglitz's holdings of more than one thousand paintings, sculptures, drawings, prints, and photographs were developed over years of activity as a dealer, a friend to artists, and, of course, a renowned photographer himself. The Philadelphia Museum of Art exhibited a large selection from that collection in 1944, in a revelatory presentation that demonstrated the evolution of such artists as O'Keeffe, Charles Demuth, Arthur Dove, Marsden Hartley, and John Marin. After Stieglitz's death in 1946, O'Keeffe decided to divide the collection among a number of institutions in order to broaden the public's opportunity to see it. The eighteen paintings and twenty-

Marcel Duchamp and Henri Marceau overseeing the installation of *The Bride Stripped Bare by Her Bachelors, Even (The Large Glass)* at the Philadelphia Museum of Art in 1954. Published in the *Philadelphia Inquirer*, July 25, 1954 (Urban Archives. Temple University, Philadelphia)

R. Sturgis Ingersoll and Mrs. Adrian Siegel with Pablo Picasso's *Man with a Lamb* in the Ingersolls' garden, 1953, photographed by Adrian Siegel
(Ingersoll Family Album. Courtesy Perry Benson, Jr.)

seven works on paper given to Philadelphia in 1949 provided the Museum with a superb representation of the distinctly American and distinctly modern vision championed by Stieglitz.

Before Philadelphia reaped these munificent gifts from a distance, a number of local citizens were filling their lives with modern art in marked advance of their city's museum. In the 1920s, an active community of artists, architects, and musicians had defied Philadelphia's image as a conservative town. The presence of figures such as the painter Arthur B. Carles and the conductor Leopold Stokowski inspired a dedicated group of cultural devotees. Like their New York counterparts, they were motivated by a bold contrarian spirit, most fiercely exemplified by Dr. Albert C. Barnes. Barnes's passion for French art extended from the paintings of Cézanne and Renoir to those of contemporaries such as Henri Matisse; he also championed the work of Pennsylvanians such as Charles Demuth and Horace Pippin. The Museum of Art did not escape Barnes's well-known scorn for official institutions, and the Barnes Foundation stands today as a monument to Barnes's independence as well as his aesthetic acumen. But despite—and sometimes because of—his contrariness, Barnes's presence cannot be underestimated for its power to catalyze Philadelphia in the pursuit of the new.

Indeed, shortly after the 1928 opening of the Museum's grand building on Fairmount, there was a marked awareness of the need to include modern art in the new institution. In 1930 a Committee on Modern Art was established to ensure that adequate space would be devoted to the work of contemporary artists. In 1933 the Museum inaugurated a series of what would be month-long exhibitions devoted to five private collections of modern art in Philadelphia. The first celebrated the collection of Miss Anna Warren Ingersoll and Mr. and Mrs. R. Sturgis Ingersoll. Mr. Ingersoll had been responsible for the Museum's first acquisition of a painting by Pablo Picasso: in 1931, as a thirty-two year old attorney, he convinced his father to contribute funds to buy *Woman with Loaves,* of 1906. Ingersoll gravitated to modern sculpture in particular, and eventually the garden of his country house in Penllyn was dotted with masterpieces such as Picasso's bronze *Man with a Lamb.* In 1958 he gave seven sculptures to the Museum.

The greatest of the early Philadelphia modernist collectors was Earl Horter, an artist who worked at the advertising agency N. W. Ayer and Son. During the course of the 1920s he built a collection particularly rich in Cubist masterworks, purchased on his frequent trips to Paris. When financial need obliged him to sell the collection piecemeal in the 1930s, the Philadelphia Museum of Art was able to acquire from Horter its first sculpture by Constantin Brancusi, the 1912 marble *Mademoiselle Pogany I.* Other objects have come back to the Museum circuitously, such as Duchamp's first version of *Nude Descending a Staircase (No. 1),* which the Arensbergs bought from Horter in 1934 and presented to the Museum in 1950.

The presence of Philadelphia collectors such as these cannot be underestimated in motivating Fiske Kimball, an architectural historian and medievalist by training, to build a major twentieth-century section for the Museum. Just over twenty years after the opening of the building, this was accomplished with breathtaking suddenness, and the Museum became an instant center in this country for modern art. In the process, the new collection assumed its own identity. At first, the Gallatin and Arensberg clusters were displayed on different floors, in recognition of their separate histories. But over time, the collections were integrated, given their natural complementarity with each other and with the Museum's other modern works of art.

In the tradition of Gallatin's original concept, a museum of "living art" shouldered an implicit obligation to grow. In the 1960s and 1970s the Museum itself, like others across the country, actively observed and explored the art of the current moment. Important individual gifts and purchases reflect the postwar shift of cultural preeminence from Paris to New York and the successive phenomena of Abstract Expressionism and Pop art. In 1961 the artist Franz Kline gave the Museum his monumental painting *Torches Mauve*. In 1965 the Museum acquired Alexander Calder's majestic mobile *Ghost*, a stunning white swirl of modernity, for the Great Stair Hall at the heart of the building. That same year the Friends of the Philadelphia Museum of Art was founded expressly for the acquisition of contemporary art, and during the course of their thirty-five-year tenure, the Friends sponsored the purchase of works of art that were often virtually brand new. Friends' purchases include such now-historic objects as Robert Rauschenberg's 1963 silkscreen painting, *Estate*, acquired in 1967. A city-wide blossoming in contemporary art events and organizations also made an impact on the Museum. In 1963 the Institute of Contemporary Art at the University of Pennsylvania was established, and its groundbreaking program included, in 1965, Andy Warhol's first museum-type exhibition. The Museum's acquisition of works by artists ranging from Warhol to Agnes Martin and Paul Thek reflects the importance of the I.C.A. as a catalyst for Philadelphia collections.

The foundation provided by the Gallatin and Arensberg collections remains a key determinant for the growth of the Museum's holdings. These collections have begun a rich dialogue that takes place within and across the galleries, and it is this ongoing dialogue that new works of art join and enrich. The subjects of conversation are many: the invention and evolution of the Readymade, the development of abstraction, the relationship of nature and technology, to name but a few. Duchamp's *Fountain*, of 1917, an ordinary urinal displayed on its back, is a necessary forerunner to Warhol's *Brillo Boxes*, painted wooden sculptures meant to look commercially "Readymade" but in fact newly fabricated by the artist. Léger's *The City* anticipates James Rosenquist's decision, almost half a century later, to develop a painting idiom based on the format of the billboard. In building the collection, we view the concept of visual influence as multidirectional and nonlinear. The Museum's galleries present a situation in which one can say not only that a painting of the 1930s by Piet Mondrian may have influenced a painting of the 1970s by Ellsworth Kelly or Gerhard Richter, but in the eyes of a contemporary viewer, the Kelly or the Richter have an equally significant impact on the Mondrian. Those crosscurrents across time and place give proof that the older work is indeed "living," and that the younger work is strong enough to flourish in such company.

The Arensberg and Gallatin collections also provide an inspiring precedent to the Museum's continuing program in the sense that they were formed in collaboration with contemporary artists. Duchamp thereafter played a large role in the Museum's presentation and display of the collection. That distinction remains a mandate for the Museum to follow, even during a period in which the art world has come to resemble a multinational industry rather than small coteries of mutual friends and advocates. Such collaborations happen in exhibitions developed in close conjunction with an artist, a tradition at the Museum dating back as far as 1948, when a major exhibition devoted to Henri Matisse could be counted as contemporary. Since then, artists ranging from Jasper Johns to Anselm Kiefer to Gabriel Orozco have become deeply involved in the development of landmark presentations of their work at this Museum. An ongoing exhibition series initiated in 1993 entitled *Museum Studies* specifically enlists artists to produce new works in response to the Museum, its program, and its collection. The series was inaugurated memorably when Sherrie Levine "re-created" Brancusi's *Newborn* by casting the Museum's marble sculpture in frosted glass, making six new sculptures that were displayed atop six grand pianos in the Great Stair Hall. Often, close involvement with the artist extends to the matter of individual acquisitions for the permanent collection, whether in choosing with Sol LeWitt a wall drawing for a vaulted ceiling or working with Cy Twombly to design a gallery with the space necessary to house a sequential and symmetric ten-part painting. The rich talent and diversity of local artists—many

Installation view with six pianos of *Museum Studies 1: Sherrie Levine* at the Philadelphia Museum of Art, 1993

Installation view of *Jonathan Borofsky* exhibition at the Philadelphia Museum of Art, 1984

first attracted by Philadelphia's excellent art schools—continue to provide an extraordinary resource for the Museum's collection and exhibition program.

The sense of daring exemplified by the Museum's individual forerunners offers paramount inspiration for the present day, a pluralistic moment at which the convictions of "isms" have faded and the dictates of taste are far from absolute. The sculptures acquired by the Museum in the last decade include materials as diverse as a human skull, papier-mâché, fruit rinds, and lightbulbs. At the same time, painting in oils on canvas—again and again presumed dead during the course of the twentieth century—remains a continuing source of surprise and provocation. We live at a time when brand new works of art often enjoy immediate and widespread acclaim, but there is no less urgent need than to make courageous choices and to keep one's eyes open for art that is far more intelligent than its appearance might initially suggest. For whatever profound and mysterious reasons, which works of art will look as young one hundred years from now as Cézanne's *Large Bathers* does today, as startling as Duchamp's Readymades, as graceful as Brancusi's *Bird in Space*? For the answers to these questions, we rely on our own eyes as well as those of passionate collectors engaged in the art of their own moment. Working together with them, the Museum can continue to grow as a collection of collections, with unique tastes and interests mutually reinforcing one another in a richly layered whole. This book salutes the eminent and generous artists and collectors of the twentieth century and anticipates with pleasure the exciting associations with those of the twenty-first.

Ann Temkin
The Muriel and Philip Berman Curator
of Modern and Contemporary Art

Twentieth Century
Painting and Sculpture
in the Philadelphia
Museum of Art

PAUL CÉZANNE (French, 1839–1906)

The Large Bathers, 1906
Oil on canvas, 82⅞ x 98¾ inches
Purchased with the W. P. Wilstach Fund

This is the last and largest work among scores of paintings of nude bathers, male and female, made by Cézanne over the course of his lifetime. The monumental scene conveys a grand sense of synthesis, combining figures and landscape in a stagelike setting of towering proportion. For both the formal structure of the landscape and the company of awkward bathers, Cézanne drew upon art historical precedents and his own imagination rather than natural observation. The painter exposed his artifice in technique as well as composition: the vibrant surface exults in rich, swirling layers of blues and greens, generously applied to make the air as palpable an element as earth and foliage.

Despite its grandeur, the painting has the feel of an unanswered question, a testament to the "anxiety" Picasso famously declared to be the source of his great interest in Cézanne. The artist left unresolved the startling contrast between the lushly painted landscape and the stiffly drawn, expressionless figures. A haunting stillness hovers over the scene, with its two mysterious figures in the background; an air of disquiet is signaled by a swimmer's interruption of the pond's calm surface. The painting's final state remains unfinished, revealed particularly in the seated figure at the lower right whose long arms betray their previous identity as two legs ready to depart the scene.

Painted at the very end of Cézanne's life, *The Large Bathers* revisits his own creative history and invokes his countless hours of studying and copying the masterpieces at the Louvre. The assembly of bathers calls to mind scenes of mythical goddesses more readily than modern French women, and the mood suggests a ritual rather than a picnic. Notwithstanding its deep roots in the past, the painting's pictorial daring is unparalleled, and today *The Large Bathers* appears as the opening scene to the artistic drama of the twentieth century.

HENRI-JULIEN-FÉLIX ROUSSEAU
(French, 1844–1910)

The Merry Jesters, 1906
Oil on canvas, 57⅜ x 44⅝ inches
The Louise and Walter Arensberg Collection

The jungle pictures Rousseau made during the last years of his life brought him the recognition he had craved since he first took up painting in the 1870s. Rousseau referred to these extraordinarily rich paintings as his "Mexican landscapes," and it was once thought that he had been to Mexico in the army of Napoleon III. It now seems certain that the exotic flora and fauna he claimed to have seen there were actually observed during his frequent visits to the Jardin des Plantes in Paris and in children's books and illustrated magazines. In *The Merry Jesters,* a group of bearded monkeys stare intensely at the viewer, as if a sudden noise has disturbed their play. One monkey, isolated in the middle distance, hugs a tree trunk in fear, while the largest of the group bares a crescent of sharp white teeth to ward off danger. The amusing creatures prod and tickle each other with a reed and what looks like a garden rake or a back-scratcher, and an overturned milk bottle suggests the denouement of their comic escapades.

The dreamy sumptuousness of the jungle is achieved through a rigid formal composition covering almost the entire canvas with an impenetrable curtain of lush vegetation. This lattice of tropical leaves and fronds, each carefully turned toward the eye to display its full shape, is painted in deliberately luminous colors. The foliage shimmers as if under stage lights. The absurd, pantomime humor of the picture is strangely at odds with the latent menace of the monkeys' unsettling stares and the frozen stillness of the scene. The tragicomic effect is typical of Rousseau's late work, which was widely celebrated by the avant-garde of the first decade of the twentieth century. This painting formerly belonged to the artists Robert and Sonia Delaunay, who sold it to Walter and Louise Arensberg in 1920.

PABLO PICASSO (Spanish, 1881–1973)

Self-Portrait, 1906
Oil on canvas, 36³⁄₁₆ x 28⁷⁄₈ inches
A. E. Gallatin Collection

This portrait is the triumphant manifesto of a twenty-five-year-old artist who, after several years of struggle to channel his innate virtuosity, resoundingly emerged with a unique voice. It was Picasso's first explicit self-portrait painting since 1901. In the intervening years, he had placed himself in his canvases only in the guise of hungry beggars or scraggly performers, metaphors for the impoverished painter scorned by bourgeois society. Here, in contrast, Picasso casts himself as a hardy, athletic figure whose carriage suggests that of a boxer or a wrestler. Drawings for the composition place a brush in Picasso's right hand, but in the final painting that hand is clenched in a fist, and a palette offers the only clue to his profession. The artist's power is concentrated in the massive right arm, which overwhelms the rest of the simply rendered body.

This is evidently a self-portrait painted in the third person, since the artist's eyes do not gaze back at a mirror image but look off into an indefinite distance. It is as if the artist wears a mask, much as an athlete or a warrior wears a helmet that signifies his power but gives no indication of his thoughts or feelings. Appearing virtually detachable, the face is separated from the artist's body both by its deep hue and by the firm demarcation of the line of the collarbone. The stylization of the exaggerated eyelids and brows, oval face, and oversized ear draw on various sources, including the inspiration of Gauguin, especially his sculpture. It also evokes the so-called primitive art that Picasso knew well at this time, including archaic Iberian sculptures on display at the Louvre and Romanesque sculptures he had seen in Spain the previous summer. Casting himself as the painter without a brush, Picasso confidently and presciently ascribes to himself the "magic" he would continue to discover and treasure in pre-modern and non-Western art traditions.

ANDRÉ DERAIN (French, 1880–1954)

Portrait of Henri Matisse, c. 1905
Oil on canvas, 13 x 16⅛ inches
A. E. Gallatin Collection

In July 1905 Derain visited Matisse in Collioure, a coastal village near the Spanish border. In contrast to the tourist escape St. Tropez, where Matisse had vacationed and painted in 1904, or the more famous resorts on the northern coast of the Mediterranean where the Impressionists worked, Collioure in 1905 was a port town and an authentic fishing village in decline. Guidebooks at the time emphasize Collioure's light and color as its most famous attractions, and letters from Derain to friends in Paris record that the rendering of light and shadow was a topic much discussed by the two artists. In their short time together they succeeded in reinventing outdoor landscape painting in an almost artlessly naive-looking style, approximating a sense of primitive directness that corresponds with their experience of this new painting locale and the brilliance of its light effects.

The portrait of Matisse is one of three images of him painted by Derain, a younger artist's representation of his older mentor and a souvenir of the summer when the two most influenced one another's art. In relation to the other works—one, a close-up of Matisse's face, and the other, a sketchy depiction of him with brushes in hand—this painting best captures their routine together and the sensations of light, sand, and sea that informed their paintings. Matisse is shown through a doorway, seated at a folding table by the sea. Barefoot, with his pants rolled up above his ankles, he sits on a flimsy beach chair. He rests his head on his hand, and his face is thrown into shadow by a broad-brimmed hat. Thick daubs of saturated pigment transform delicate dots of pointillism into a bold style of individual brushstrokes placed side-by-side or one above the other. The result is a mosaic-like pattern and a rhythmic scheme of primary colors that maintain the freshness of a rapid sketch while vividly capturing the setting where Matisse and Derain worked.

ALEXY JAWLENSKY (Russian, active Germany, 1864–1941)

Portrait, 1912
Oil on cardboard, 21⅛ x 19½ inches
The Louise and Walter Arensberg Collection

Jawlensky's innovative reinterpretations of the conventions for depicting the human face made a distinct imprint on modern portraiture. His approach reflects the search for authentic new forms of self-expression, a vital tenet of early modern art that would inform the artist's paintings throughout his long career. Jawlensky developed an inventive, offbeat sense of color and a painting style that consciously appears naive and untrained. Like his friend Wassily Kandinsky, a fellow Russian émigré to Munich, Jawlensky invested color with mystical power. This portrait, a schematic depiction of the model's prominent features, thick eyebrows, large eyes, and voluptuous lips, reveals his ability to magnify and distort appearances through the intuitive use of color combinations and painterly marks.

The sitter was Jawlensky's model many times in 1911 and 1912, although her identity has never been pinpointed. The artist chose to exclude clues to her inner psychology or social identity, such as jewelry or clothing, and her image is unified with its background by enclosure within the square canvas, intensified by consistent patterns of energetic brushstrokes. The moody effect of the whole reinforces the theatricality of Jawlensky's image of archetypal feminine mystery. His rendering of the woman's brilliantly colored purple lips, shadowed eyes, and white and red cheeks intensifies the masklike qualities produced by cosmetics and creates a coloristic dissonance tinged with unsettling emotions.

FRANTIŠEK KUPKA (Czech, active France, 1871–1957)

Disks of Newton (Study for "Fugue in Two Colors"), 1912
Oil on canvas, 39½ x 29 inches
The Louise and Walter Arensberg Collection

When the Czech painter Kupka exhibited his purely abstract paintings at the 1912 Salon d'Automne in Paris, the French critics were enraged. The blazing colors and cosmic symbolism of works such as *Disks of Newton* were seen as a blatant challenge to French taste and tradition. The title refers to the seventeenth-century English physicist Sir Isaac Newton, who discovered that the light of the sun is made up of the seven colors of the spectrum: red, orange, yellow, green, blue, indigo, and violet. Newton expressed the mixing of these colors in the form of a disk, or a color wheel, which showed that if two different colors of the spectrum are combined, they produce a third color, and if all seven colors are mixed optically, they produce white.

Kupka's radiant composition uses Newton's scientific discoveries by incorporating circular bands of expanding concentric rings of burning, vibrating color, including the full range of the spectrum, along with white. The forms overlap and interpenetrate each other to produce an exciting sense of spinning movement. The artist's fascination with cosmology and astronomy suggests that the circular blades of color whirling out from the red center may relate to images of the planets and their orbits. Another analogy is demonstrated by the word *fugue* in the second half of the title, which evokes the polyphonic interweaving in musical arrangements of Johann Sebastian Bach. Kupka believed that painting should be as abstract as music, declaring: "I can find something between sight and hearing and I can produce a fugue in colors as Bach has done in music."[†]

ROBERT DELAUNAY (French, 1855–1941)

St. Séverin, 1909
Oil on canvas, 38 x 27½ inches
The Louise and Walter Arensberg Collection

Between the spring of 1909 and early 1910,
St. Séverin, a small thirteenth-century Gothic church
near Delaunay's Paris studio, inspired seven of his
paintings. In each Delaunay explored a new pictorial
composition, taking subtly different angles toward
the church and varying the intensity of the color or
the richness of architectural detail. As a group, the
St. Séverin paintings show that Delaunay was con-
sistently drawn to explore the interaction of light, color,
and space in the cavernous church interior and its
architecture of twisting columns and pointed arches.
Transforming the prismatic color he observed refracted
through stained-glass windows into images of forms
dematerialized by light, the artist arrived at a language
of visual fragmentation much more expressive than
other variations of Cubism then taking hold among
advanced artists in Paris.

In this painting, the fourth in the series, the darkly
shadowed bays of St. Séverin create a dramatic
recession into space arrested by the contrasting
bright yellow windows at the center of the picture.
This rhythmic oscillation between surface and depth
produces a kaleidoscopic sensation of shifting perspectives and light. On the reverse side of this work is
a composition that inaugurates another important
thematic series Delaunay painted before World War I:
The Eiffel Tower. The Tower, an international symbol of
modernity, and the old Gothic church of St. Séverin
became the subjects of Delaunay's painting at nearly
the same moment. This coincidence reflects ideas
about the early history of modern architecture in
France, where Gothic architectural principles were
celebrated as precursors of the structural innovations
announced by the Tower of iron and glass.

PABLO PICASSO (Spanish, 1881–1973)

Man with a Violin, 1912
Oil on canvas, 39⅜ x 28¹³⁄₁₆ inches
The Louise and Walter Arensberg Collection

Between 1907 and 1914 Picasso's art evolved as if it were a secret language being invented in private conversation with his close collaborator Georges Braque. *Man with a Violin* reflects the state of their nearly day-to-day interchange in 1912, a time when their styles became almost indistinguishable, based on a shared vocabulary of gridlike scaffolding, overlapping planes, and a palette of ocher, white, and gray. As Braque and Picasso gauged how their paintings evolved, and sometimes even jockeyed competitively to innovate new methods, the two never veered from the rigorously disciplined but intuitive approach that led them to create such focused series of works.

Man with a Violin dates from the spring or summer of 1912, a period in the evolution of Cubism often described as hermetic, as the connection between what appears in Braque's and Picasso's paintings and objects recognizable in nature is almost completely severed. This picture cannot be compared to the outward appearance of anything already known or seen, but instead creates a reality according to its own logic of seeing and reading. Immediately eye-catching and absorbing, its interwoven, shimmering facets and semitransparent planes juxtapose a skeletal, linear structure and transform the receding grid of perspectival space into a flat pattern. A monumental pyramidal form evokes a human presence, while other clues suggest strands of hair, a moustache, and ears. Two F-shaped sound holes are the only signs of a violin, and scroll-like shapes at the bottom left suggest the arm of a chair. Paintings such as *Man with a Violin* paved the way for much abstract art to come, but Picasso's persistent inclusion of abbreviated signs for human physiognomy and objects shows what all his subsequent work confirms: he was more interested in dissecting and reinventing representation than in pursuing pure abstraction.

MARCEL DUCHAMP (American, born France, 1887–1968)

Nude Descending a Staircase (No. 2), 1912
Oil on canvas, 57⅞ x 35⅛ inches
The Louise and Walter Arensberg Collection

Duchamp's *Nude Descending a Staircase (No. 2)* sparked a storm of controversy at the International Exhibition of Modern Art held at the National Guard 69th Regiment Armory in New York in 1913. The painting was perceived by the majority of art critics to be utterly unintelligible, and it soon became the butt of jokes, jingles, and caricatures. The *American Art News* offered a ten dollar reward to the first reader who could "find the lady"† within the jumble of inter-locking planes and jagged lines, and newspaper cartoonists had a field day with the painting, lampooning it with such titles as "The Rude Descending the Staircase (Rush Hour at the Subway)" and the memorable "Explosion in a Shingle Factory." When Duchamp learned of the scandal, he was delighted, and the widespread notoriety that the painting brought him encouraged the French artist to move to New York two years later.

Duchamp reduced the descending nude to a series of some twenty different static positions whose fractured volumes and linear panels fill almost the entire canvas. The faceted disintegration of the mechanized figure and the monochromatic tonality are typical of Cubist painting of the time. However, the serial depiction of movement goes beyond Cubism in its attempt to map the motion and energy of the body as it passes through space. Duchamp's interest in plotting the static phases of a moving subject has often been compared to the work of the Italian Futurists, who were obsessed with notions of velocity. Another precedent for the work can be found in the time-lapse photography of Étienne-Jules Marey in France and Eadweard Muybridge and Thomas Eakins in the United States. Muybridge's book *Animal Locomotion,* of 1887, which included a sequence of twenty-four images of a naked woman descending a flight of stairs, possibly served as a source for Duchamp's landmark painting.

RAYMOND DUCHAMP-VILLON
(French, 1876–1918)

The Lovers, 1913
Plaster, 27 x 39⅝ x 5¼ inches
Gift of the family of the artist

The Lovers is a dramatic exploration of Cubist principles in the arena of sculpture. Its volumes and rhythms contain echoes of the Western tradition carried from antiquity to nineteenth-century artists such as Auguste Rodin, and the erotic subject matter is both timeless and universal. But its starkly chiseled forms and deliberately awkward grace make the sculpture unmistakably modern. Duchamp-Villon

transformed the pair of lovers into an abstract composition that subordinates the elaboration of details to a sense of balletic harmony.

The artist's choice of a deep relief format reflects his embrace of Cubism as a program for a complete environment, leading beyond painting to sculpture and architecture. He wed the avant-garde notions of his artistic circle with the classical ideal of the integration of the arts into daily life. Duchamp-Villon was committed to the development of a practice of monumental public sculpture as well as the modernization of ornamental carving for architectural interiors and facades. Assumed to be the last of five plaster works on this theme, *The Lovers* relates to several medallion reliefs

of birds and animals that Duchamp-Villon made specifically for architectural settings.

When Duchamp-Villon died of typhoid fever in 1918 at the age of forty-two, the realization of his artistic ambitions had already been postponed by his years as a medical officer in World War I. However, he left a strong legacy as a pioneer of Cubist sculpture and theory, and a studio filled with plasters awaiting further development or casting in bronze. The family of Marcel Duchamp, the sculptor's younger brother and great admirer, ultimately donated many of these precious works in plaster to the Philadelphia Museum of Art, a gift that makes the Museum a center for Duchamp-Villon's work in the United States.

JACQUES VILLON (GASTON DUCHAMP)
(French, 1875–1963)

Young Girl, 1912
Oil on canvas, 57⁹/₁₆ x 45 inches
The Louise and Walter Arensberg Collection

The Duchamp household into which Jacques Villon
was born in 1875 produced more than its fair share
of creative talent, with four of the seven children
destined for careers in the visual arts. Gaston
Duchamp marked his decision to become an artist
by changing his name to Jack (later Jacques) Villon,
after the medieval French poet François Villon. He
was the eldest of the four artists, who also included
his brothers Raymond and Marcel and a sister
Suzanne. Villon devoted the first fifteen years of his
career to graphic work, producing prints and caricatures for weekly newspapers and illustrated journals.
Around 1910 he became attracted to the intellectual
possibilities of Cubist painting; his musical concept
of color construction, however, distinguishes his
early paintings from the somber canvases of Braque
and Picasso. Villon described himself as the
"Impressionist of Cubism," and his best paintings
from this period create a unity of form, color, and
composition through light and lyricism.

Painted in the same year that Villon helped to organize
the "Section d'Or" (Golden Section) exhibition at the
Galerie La Boétie in Paris, *Young Girl* is a portrait of
the artist's younger sister Yvonne, then twenty-three
years old, seated in an armchair. The systematic
geometry of the picture relates directly to the artist's
efforts to base the language of Cubist painting on
mathematical proportion corresponding to the Golden
Section, in which the ratio of the smaller part to the
larger is the same as the ratio of the larger part to
the whole. The entire composition is constructed out
of small, volumetric pyramids, a technique that Villon
evolved from a description in Leonardo da Vinci's
Treatise on Painting, which had only recently been
translated into French. The rounded forms of the
sitter, her facial features and dainty feet, emerge from
within the dense network of triangles. The superimposed planes of rich colors illuminate the canvas
with a crystalline light.

WASSILY KANDINSKY (Russian, active Germany, 1866–1944)

Improvisation No. 29 (The Swan), 1912
Oil on canvas, 41¾ x 38³⁄₁₆ inches
The Louise and Walter Arensberg Collection

Kandinsky initially found the subject matter of his paintings in the folk art and fairytales of his native Russia and of Germany, his adopted country, especially in the landscape around Munich, where he lived and worked from 1896 to 1914. In 1909 he began to free color, shape, and line from the constraints of describing objects or suggesting readable narratives, increasingly dissolving the contours that separated discrete images in his pictures. Music was the prototype he adopted as he envisaged the possibility of abstract painting compositions organized to balance the allusive and the recognizable. Articulating these ideas in his treatise *Concerning the Spiritual in Art,* written the same year he completed *Improvisation No. 29 (The Swan),* Kandinsky carefully considered the equilibrium of abstraction and representation in his work.

The musical analogy informed the way Kandinsky categorized his paintings, as Impressions, Improvisations, or Compositions, depending on the degrees of spontaneity and description they balanced. *Improvisation No. 29 (The Swan),* one of many Improvisations Kandinsky painted between 1908 and 1917, reads as a pulsating abstraction created from subtle color harmonies delicately applied in a manner that derives from the artist's experience working in watercolor. Within its assortment of invented forms and marks, it is possible to discern landscape elements such as plants and stones in the foreground and the presence of birds on the left. The artist's use of aerial perspective eliminates the horizon, flattening and distorting observed nature while also unifying the composition with an overall organic vibrancy. Whether or not the artist intended the subliminal, symbolic imagery to be decoded by the viewer—even as he hailed the revelatory power generated by pure form and color—is one of the abiding mysteries of Kandinsky's pre–World War I painting.

MARC CHAGALL (French, born Belorussia, 1887–1985)

Half-Past Three (The Poet), 1911
Oil on canvas, 77 ⅛ x 57 inches
The Louise and Walter Arensberg Collection

Half-Past Three (The Poet) belongs to the group of monumental, euphoric paintings that Chagall produced in the months following his arrival in Paris from art school in Saint Petersburg. The blue poet sits at his red table, green head upturned on neckless shoulders, rooted in the ordered chaos of his environment. Chagall's fragmentation of the body and background into fractured planes and diagonal shafts of color imbues the composition with a prismatic sensation, as if the poet inhabited the magic space of a kaleidoscope. The painting reflects Chagall's strong sympathy with the painters Robert and Sonia Delaunay, whose so-called Orphic paintings were structured with bright and luminous color, far removed from the somber palette of Picasso and Braque's Cubism, and surely reminding Chagall of the folk art of his native Russia. The palette of blue, green, red, violet, and icy white—charted in his vertical signature—creates an overall unity that embraces vivid details like the flowers on the curtain and the utensils on the table.

Amid the relatively inexpressive landscapes and still lifes of Cubism, the lyrical sentiment of Chagall's compositions was initially criticized as too "poetic." Indeed, in his first years in Paris, he moved in a literary circle, counting among his closest friends the poets Guillaume Apollinaire and Blaise Cendrars. The figure portrayed here serves as an ode to the muses: coffee cup in hand, feline temptress by his side, friendly wine bottle tipped at the ready. The poet's notebook, with Cyrillic phrases from a love poem, doubles as a palette, with its stripes of color opposite the writing. This delightfully tumultuous image of artistic inspiration persuasively suggests an indirect self-portrait.

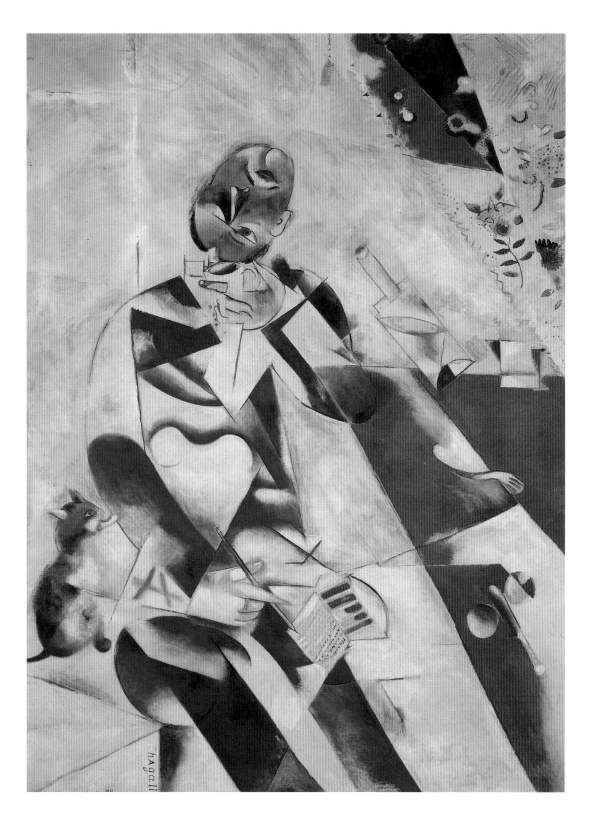

ALEXANDER PORFIREVICH ARCHIPENKO
(American, born Ukraine, 1887–1964)

The Bather, 1915
Oil, graphite, paper, and metal on panel,
20 x 11½ inches
The Louise and Walter Arensberg Collection

The Bather is a tour de force among the low-relief
"sculpto-paintings" that Archipenko began constructing
in 1914. The artist used the principle of Cubist collage
to create a synthesis of painting and sculpture in these
polychrome compositions. Archipenko was among
the few sculptors to be attracted by Cubism, and the
angular fragmentation of planes and transposition of
concave and convex forms in this work can be
compared to similar painted motifs in the work of
Braque and Picasso. The elongated female bather of
the title is composed of two cone-shaped sheets of
flattened metal, which Archipenko wedged together
and painted a glowing orange that suffuses the entire
panel with a soft golden light. The artist made this
work in Nice, where he spent the war years, and his
preoccupation with intense color and light can be seen
as a direct result of his stay in this sun-drenched
Mediterranean resort.

Archipenko incorporated a large range of materials
and found objects into his sculpto-paintings, such as
sheet metal, wood, fabric, tin, glass, plaster, metal
foil, and photographs. These materials were superimposed on a painted panel, introducing a textural
variety of complex pictorial effects, including trans-
parency and reflection. The unexpected, often disquiet-
ing shifts from projecting volume to flat surface—here
between the conical figure and the delicately shaded
classical column beside her—enhance the machine-
age dynamism of the piece, while the imposition of
luminous color intensifies the optical effects of the
forms to a degree that makes traditional sculpture
seem dull. As Archipenko later explained: "Here I rendered the shape of a figure stepping out of the water
with a column nearby. The form is yellow, the water
blue. How absurd it would have been if I had
attempted to carve the color of the water and the
color of the figure."[†]

ALBERT GLEIZES (French, 1881–1953)

Man on a Balcony (Portrait of Dr. Morinaud), 1912
Oil on canvas, 77 x 45¼ inches
The Louise and Walter Arensberg Collection

Man on a Balcony is an open declaration of the
principles of Cubist painting. It was completed the
same year that Gleizes co-authored a book on Cubism
with the painter Jean Metzinger. The composition
demonstrates the Cubist style of broken lines and
fractured planes as applied to a traditional format of
painting. Gleizes's rendering of the tall, elegantly
posed man leaning gracefully against a balustrade
dominates the foreground of the painting, where the
figure inhabits a readable space bathed in natural light.
Competing with this monumental, three-dimensional
presence is the pattern of perpendicular lines and
scalloped arcs that produce a virtual diagram of the
angles of the man's body and anatomy.

This structure evolves into a complicated cityscape
of clouds, windows, chimneys, train tracks, and
bridges behind the contemplative figure. Suggestive
of the air, the space, and even the passage of time
between these places are bubblelike shapes that
emanate from the man to the animated urban pano-
rama behind him. Gleizes's vocabulary becomes
more experimental as he captures the cacophony
and simultaneity of modern city life using a vocabulary
of abbreviated, invented signs. The gray, ocher,
beige, and brown colors, often identified with the rigor
of Cubist thought, suggest the grimy, smoky city atmosphere, although Gleizes has enlivened this neutral
palette by including bright greens and reds as well as
creamy white highlights. The large size of the painting
contrasts with the intimately scaled Cubist works of
Picasso and Braque, reflecting the destination Gleizes
envisioned for his work: the public "salons" of Paris,
where he exhibited in the hope of bringing Cubism
to wider audiences.

JUAN GRIS (Spanish, 1887–1927)

Still Life Before an Open Window, Place Ravignan, 1915
Oil on canvas, 45⅝ x 35 inches
The Louise and Walter Arensberg Collection

Gris's *Still Life Before an Open Window, Place Ravignan* reveals the artist at the height of his powers, expertly balancing lyricism and geometric rigor in a composition of evocative spatial juxtapositions and luxurious color. Its harmonious balance of dense pockets of animated, fractured space and flat areas of simplicity and tranquillity reflects Gris's talent and experience as a brilliant maker of Cubist collages. The resplendent colors and subject, a view through his studio to an open window and the street, hint at Gris's recent friendship with Henri Matisse and the mutual exchange that shaped both artists' work at this time. Gris's innovations lie in his extension of the Cubist premise of interlacing planes to encompass the relation of interior and exterior spaces.

In rendering the indoor still life, Gris elided distinctions between a compote, glasses, a wine bottle, a newspaper, and a book. The table is meticulously painted to imitate wood graining. This detail makes reference to the trompe l'oeil painting and pasted papers in Picasso's and Braque's Cubist works. But whereas those elements often float independently from objects in their paintings and collages, Gris reasserted the connection between the pattern and the table to which it adheres. The word "journal," elongated to rhyme with the faceted striations on a water jug, is but one indicator of the elasticity of signs and objects in the picture. The flat, repeating arabesque pattern of the balustrade links the plane of the still life and that of the building facade, railing, and streetlight. The blue light bathing this distant scene suffuses its taut formal dynamics and visual compression with a dreamy softness, as does the inclusion of an unexpected natural element, a canopy of trees, to frame the composition.

HENRI MATISSE (French, 1869–1954)

Mademoiselle Yvonne Landsberg, 1914
Oil on canvas, 58 x 38⅜ inches
The Louise and Walter Arensberg Collection

This painting overturns assumptions about an artist
best known for his bright and joyous view of the world.
The portrait is from a period between 1913 and 1917
during which Matisse produced paintings of remarkable somberness and austerity. Nevertheless, these
works share a daring level of pictorial innovation that
makes them among the most powerful of his
long career.

The history of this painting began with a portrait
drawing of Yvonne Landsberg commissioned in the
spring of 1914 by her family, affluent Brazilians living
in Paris. Yvonne's brother, an acquaintance of Matisse
and an enthusiast of his work, proposed the idea.
Evidently Matisse was intrigued by the young girl he
was drawing, and he asked the family if he could
make an oil painting of Yvonne. The work was carried
out over the period of a few months, ending when
the Landsberg women returned to Brazil in August
shortly before the outbreak of World War I.

The process of making the portrait involved a long
series of sittings, always attended by Yvonne's
brother. Several drawings emerged during the course
of the process, and various versions of the painting
were done as well, which Matisse continually painted
over in order to begin anew. Only during the final
sitting did the artist reverse his brush and use its
wooden end to scratch the wide, curving lines that
radiate from the shoulders and hips of his subject.
The force of these arcs dominates the portrayal,
metaphorically likening the demure young woman
to a budding flower. The heart-shaped lines seem to
project an energy that her body cannot yet accom-
modate and suggest the state of becoming that
defines adolescence. Perhaps the portrait was too
daring for the Landsbergs, who chose not to acquire
it. The painting was sent to an exhibition in New York,
where Louise and Walter Arensberg purchased it
in 1915.

DANIEL GARBER (American, 1880–1958)

Quarry, Evening, 1913
Oil on canvas, 50 x 60 inches
Purchased with the W. P. Wilstach Fund

Quarry, Evening is a majestic portrayal of the landscape along the Delaware River near the town of New Hope, Pennsylvania, an important artists' colony during the first half of the twentieth century. Garber was one of its leading figures, having settled in the nearby village of Lumberville in 1907. A native of Indiana, Garber came to Philadelphia in 1899 to study at the Pennsylvania Academy of the Fine Arts, where he maintained a lifelong affiliation that evolved from pupil to professor. He spent the winters in Philadelphia, but the Delaware River Valley north of the city provided the heart and soul of his painting.

The New Hope artists have often been called the Pennsylvania Impressionists. Indeed, Garber had encountered the Parisians' work firsthand during his travels in Europe and shared their fascination for the fleeting effects of light. *Quarry, Evening* records a moment when the setting sun casts its glow across the upper ledges of the cliffs, leaving the ridge of trees above in deep purple shadow. Painting from direct observation outdoors, Garber faithfully captured the reflections of the cliffs in the water and the subtleties of the foliage glimmering in the dusk. However, the order and precision of Garber's approach differ distinctly from the Impressionists' interest in the accidental moment; his ideal of a sublime nature bears closer affinities to the tradition of the great nineteenth-century American landscape painters. Garber's desire to portray the glory of nature is reflected in his decision to paint the imposing quarry, a dramatic exception to the intimately scaled Delaware River landscape. The picture is nearly devoid of human presence, save for the tiny figures at work in the field. Their insignificance, like that of the small buildings in the middle distance, magnifies the awe-inspiring grandeur of the towering landscape beyond.

ARTHUR BEECHER CARLES
(American, 1882–1952)

Steichen's Garden, c. 1921
Oil on canvas, 24⅞ x 24⅛ inches
The Samuel S. White 3rd and Vera White Collection

Carles's breakthrough to a modern mode of painting was far removed from the training he received at the Pennsylvania Academy of the Fine Arts in Philadelphia. Like many American artists at the beginning of the twentieth century, his inspiration came in the form of periodic visits to France. This painting hails from a stay of several months in 1921–22, made possible with funds from his devoted patrons and a leave of absence from his position as a professor at the Pennsylvania Academy. The small, square composition portrays the graceful approach to Carles's temporary residence abroad: the home of the American photographer and painter Edward Steichen in the village of Voulangis, thirty miles east of Paris. He and Steichen had met during Carles's first trip to Paris in 1905 and became lifelong friends. Steichen served as the European scout for Gallery 291, Alfred Stieglitz's avant-garde art gallery in New York, and in 1912 Steichen convinced Stieglitz to offer Carles his first exhibition.

By the eloquent means of its radiant palette, *Steichen's Garden* communicates the relaxed pleasure Carles ex-perienced while painting in France. As a young man, the artist had proven a quick convert to the new princi-ples of color espoused by Matisse. Matisse inspired Carles to use hues of remarkable intensity in unex-pected combinations, whether in tightly composed still lifes or pure abstractions. Here the palette mingles beautiful blues and greens in the shadowy foreground and turns to pinks and yellows in the sunny distance. Carles renounced outline and detail, and articulated his forms in broad patches of color. Particularly in the delicately pale sky, the paint application is as loose and thin as that of a watercolor.

JOHN SLOAN (American, 1871–1951)

Three A.M., 1909
Oil on canvas, 32⅛ x 26¼ inches
Gift of Mrs. Cyrus McCormick

Sloan was a pioneer in the reformulation of urban
iconography and the revised ideal of feminine beauty
that characterized much of new American art at the
turn of the twentieth century. Sloan, a native of
Philadelphia and initially an illustrator for the
Philadelphia Inquirer, moved to New York City in 1904.
There he joined other artists such as Robert Henri,
William Glackens, and George Bellows in an effort to
portray the gritty reality of modern city life with humor
and pathos. The group would become known as "The
Eight" for an eight-man show organized in 1908 at the
Macbeth Gallery in New York as a protest to the
conservative ideology of the National Academy of
Design. Many years later, Sloan would be among the
handful of artists from this era retrospectively dubbed
"The Ashcan School" for their preference for the grimy
subjects of Manhattan's industrial age.

Sloan based this painting on a late-night view from his
Chelsea studio into the window of his neighbors. The
palette of warm browns and greens envelops his
subjects in a private domestic setting. The woman at
the stove stands absorbed in the quiet activity of
preparing a small meal, smoking as she listens to
the animated chatter of her friend. The proximity of
the seated figure to the open door and her extrava-
gantly plumed hat identify her with the bustle of the
outside world and provide a contrast to the domestic
intimacy represented by the woman cooking in a
nightgown and bare feet. In an era of wasp-waisted
Gibson girls, Sloan's full-figured woman evokes the
robustness of the working class and a more earthy
sexuality. The title of the painting reflects an entry in
Sloan's journal for April 28, 1909: "A good day's
work, painting on the subject that has been stewing
in my mind for some weeks. I have been watching a
curious two room household, two women and, I think,
two men, their day begins after midnight, they cook
at 3 A.M."[†]

LOUIS MICHEL EILSHEMIUS
(American, 1864–1941)

Jealousy, c. 1915
Oil on cardboard, 21⅞ x 30 inches
Gift of Mr. and Mrs. Henry Clifford

The surcharged sexual tension of *Jealousy* is typical of Eilshemius's obsessive late work, which is characterized by dramatic scenes of passion and disaster tinged with an atmosphere of pent-up violence. The artist described his life at this time as "merely a semblance of a series of nightmares diluted very faintly with a parsimony of shortest delights."[†] This strange fantasy showing a young man assailed by three women in a brothel-like interior communicates the artist's sense of isolation and despondency. The hallucinatory scene is reminiscent of the macabre tales of Edgar Allan Poe or Washington Irving, an analogy also suggested by the diaphanous shift worn by the woman advancing from the left, which gives her the appearance of a ghostly apparition. The Art Nouveau decorative device of the frame-within-a-frame dramatically focuses our attention on the suffering of the male protagonist, who lies helpless on the floor as the femmes fatales tempt, tease, and terrorize him with a dagger. The flamelike lighting of the bedroom heightens the heated atmosphere of the unfolding drama.

Eilshemius spent the first thirty-five years of his career as an artist working in obscurity before finally giving up painting in 1921, frustrated at the lack of recognition his highly idiosyncratic paintings received. The rejection of his work by the exhibition committee of the 1913 Armory Show has been cited as the catalyst for his unexpected late style. The crudely painted romantic dreamscapes the artist made over the next eight years reveal a mind in torment, haunted by floating phantasmagorical nudes, whose lack of studied anatomy and implicit eroticism earned the praise of Marcel Duchamp, one of the artist's few supporters in his final years of solitude and neglect.

CLAUDE MONET (French, 1840–1926)

Nympheas, Japanese Bridge, 1918–26
Oil on canvas, 35 x 36½ inches
The Albert M. Greenfield and Elizabeth M.
Greenfield Collection

The elaborate water garden that the Impressionist painter Claude Monet created at Giverny, a sleepy village along the river Seine some forty miles northwest of Paris, has become one of the great pilgrimage sites of modern art. The main attraction for visitors is the Japanese footbridge spanning the water-lily pond in the lower garden, which first appeared in the

artist's work in 1895. Monet returned to the motif in the famous series of water lilies that he painted during the summers of 1899 and 1900, shifting his focus from the arched bridge to the floating plants shimmering in the light. Monet reworked the theme of the Japanese bridge in the last years of his life but with vastly different results. These tumultuous late canvases display vivid coloration, expressive brushwork, and formal dissolution, such that the outlines of the bridge are barely distinguishable from the hanging plants above and the water beneath.

The gestural handling and pyrotechnics of color place this undated painting among the group of Japanese

bridge pictures that Monet painted after 1918. Compared to the harmonious order of the bridge paintings from the turn of the century, these late works exude a breathtaking sense of daring. The artist's innovations were, in part, prompted by the appearance of the bridge itself. A trellis with trailing Chinese and Japanese wisteria was added about 1910, and within a few years the footbridge was nearly hidden by a mass of hanging vines and leaves that cloaks its canopy and uprights. Here the wisteria-festooned bridge, water lilies, irises, reeds, and reflections are depicted with intensely toned pigments that coat the surface in thick layers suggestive of lavish vegetation.

PIERRE BONNARD (French, 1867–1947)

After the Shower, 1914
Oil on canvas, 37 3/8 x 26 3/16 inches
The Louis E. Stern Collection

Bonnard was one of the great colorists of twentieth-century French painting. With its gorgeous palette and dazzling optical effects, *After the Shower* is a fine illustration of what the artist meant when he claimed that painting is "the transcription of the adventures of the optic nerve."[†] The shimmering forms, dissolved in particles of light, slowly take shape before our very eyes. This canvas belongs to a celebrated series of pictures in which the artist's lifelong companion Marthe de Méligny is observed following her daily routine of washing and drying herself. These intimate portraits, drenched in sunlight and saturated with a mood of reverie, evoke the quiet life the two shared in the South of France. Bonnard's variations on the theme of Marthe's bathing ritual may have been prompted by Degas's taboo-breaking depictions of women in their own domestic surroundings washing themselves.

In this painting, Bonnard depicts his future wife with extraordinary tenderness as she sits in a chair, wrapped in a dressing gown. On the table in front of her is a glistening still-life arrangement, and to her right a white towel is draped over a stand, presumably left there to dry in the morning sunlight streaming through the window above. Marthe is shown with her eyes shut in self-absorption as she delicately dries her ankle. Bonnard captured a moment of great intimacy in this luminous picture, characteristically combining painterly beauty with psychological insight.

GIORGIO DE CHIRICO (Italian, born Greece, 1888–1978)

The Soothsayer's Recompense, 1913
Oil on canvas, 53⅜ x 70⅞ inches
The Louise and Walter Arensberg Collection

The Soothsayer's Recompense is one of a series of melancholy cityscapes that de Chirico painted shortly before World War I. These enigmatic images of deserted Italian piazzas hemmed in by arcaded buildings and seen in exaggerated perspective use a clear, sharp style to evoke a troubling dream reality. De Chirico described these thinly painted, luminous works as "metaphysical," meaning "beyond the physical." In this painting, an antique statue is situated within a deeply shadowed and eerily silent city square; its

mysterious empty spaces are suffused with a sense of loneliness and foreboding. The pictorial space is neatly bisected by what appears to be an imposing railway station and a wall that stretches across the piazza, giving the work a stagelike quality that denies real space and recalls, rather, the transcendent spaces one has dreamed or imagined. The sandy foreground is the realm of immobility and quiet, while the area beyond the low brick wall—and partially hidden by it—suggests activity and movement as a locomotive runs along the horizon, sending a billowing cloud of smoke in its wake.

The antique statue dominating the foreground of the painting represents the sleeping Ariadne, who according to Greek mythology was abandoned by her lover on the desert island of Naxos. De Chirico juxtaposed

the classical statue with the puffing steam train behind it to create a dreamlike hybrid of ancient and modern worlds, resulting in a disturbingly ambiguous sense of time and place. The long, cast shadows indicate a low, late-afternoon sun, while the mackerel sky suggests twilight. Curiously enough, however, the clock on the pediment of the colonnaded building shows the time as shortly before two o'clock.

AMEDEO MODIGLIANI (Italian, 1884–1920)

Portrait of a Polish Woman, 1919
Oil on canvas, 39½ x 25½ inches
The Louis E. Stern Collection

In the short time he was in Paris from the winter of
1906 until his death in 1920 at the age of thirty-six,
Modigliani lived as the consummate Bohemian artist,
suffering hardship to achieve ambitious artistic goals.
Famous for his temper, his passionate love affairs,
and his severe poverty, Modigliani's life and tragic
death are an extreme example of the struggle that
afflicted many of the émigré artists in Paris. Arriving
from his home in Livorno, Italy, he lived in Montmartre
and then Montparnasse, where he excelled in painting
portraits and female nudes. Stemming from an interest in African sculpture, his contact with the sculptor
Constantin Brancusi, and his own ventures in direct
stone carving, Modigliani fashioned a distinctive
approach to painting idealized images of feminine
beauty, attracting the attention of dealers by 1916.

This portrait was painted one year before he died,
when his favorite female sitters, other than his
companion Jeanne Hebuterne, were drawn from the
circle of his dealer Leopold Zborowska. Typical of
Modigliani's stylized approach to his subjects, the
monumental figure, composed of a series of graceful
arabesques including rounded shoulders, an elongated
neck, and curving arms, is situated in relation to a
spare, geometric, architectural setting. The composition is sensitively designed to calibrate the signs of
her individuality and personality with abstract pictorial
values. Pencil drawing beneath the delicately painted
surface carves through broad areas of subtly modu-
lated, flat color to outline her almond-shaped eyes and
chic coiffure. Modigliani has rendered her gently tilting
head, plunging neckline, and oversized collar in an
elegant, modern portrait that conveys the exotic
beauty and rarified taste of his subject.

CONSTANTIN BRANCUSI (French, born Romania, 1876–1957)

Bird in Space, 1924
Polished bronze with black marble base, height with base 56½ inches
The Louise and Walter Arensberg Collection

The Kiss, 1916
Limestone, height 23 inches
The Louise and Walter Arensberg Collection

Bird in Space (Yellow Bird), 1923–24?
Yellow marble with marble, limestone, and oak base, height with base 103 inches
The Louise and Walter Arensberg Collection

Mademoiselle Pogany III, 1931
White marble with four-part base of limestone and oak, height with base 50½ inches
The Louise and Walter Arensberg Collection

The work of Brancusi redefined sculpture for a new century. Born in Romania but living in Paris after 1904, Brancusi aimed to develop a sculptural idiom that looked absolutely modern. His work moved beyond the verisimilitude and melodrama exemplified by the vastly popular sculpture of Auguste Rodin. Brancusi sought inspiration in ancient, folk, and exotic precedents that preceded or bypassed the classical Western tradition of sculpture. This brought Brancusi to simplified forms, reduction of details, and hand carving of materials. *The Kiss,* for example, presents a symbolic rendering of a male and a female body merging into one. The anatomical forms of the couple are subordinated to the contours of the block of stone. But it is inaccurate to echo the artist in calling his sculptures simple: nothing could be more complicated than the dramatic contrasts between the rough-hewn wooden bases and the elegant marble or bronze sculptures atop them, the calculated effects of the reflections of light, and the subtle nuances in carving that evoke facial features and other characteristics.

As Brancusi's career continued, he worked with an ever-growing penchant for stylistic schematization and freedom from detail. In the twenty-year span from the first carving of *Mademoiselle Pogany* to the third and final version, the model's facial features virtually disappear, her arms become a single fin, and her chignon hairstyle a scalloped cascade strongly reminiscent of contemporary architecture and design. The aspect of portraiture remains, however, as Brancusi persuasively conveys the sense of Margit Pogany's exotically deep-set eyes and reserved demeanor.

The theme of the bird constitutes Brancusi's lifelong obsession, a subject he would explore in more than thirty marble and bronze versions over the course of four decades. The extreme reduction of detail that Brancusi evolved for his *Bird in Space* provoked the most notorious public misunderstanding of the artist's work. In 1926 a U.S. customs official insisted on labeling a version of the sculpture as a "miscellaneous household good" rather than a work of art, which would be tax-exempt for importation. After a long courtroom battle, the presiding judge stated that "while some difficulty might be encountered in associating it with a bird, it is nevertheless pleasing to look at and highly ornamental," and he ruled in Brancusi's favor. The dramatically long, slim sculptures represent Brancusi's idea of the essence of a bird, rather than a natural likeness; a slanting oval plane represents the head and beak, and a flared footing creates the powerful upward force that lifts the bird "in space."

MARSDEN HARTLEY (American, 1877–1943)

Painting No. 4 (A Black Horse), 1915
Oil on canvas with painted frame, 39¼ x 31⅝ inches
The Alfred Stieglitz Collection

An early work the artist painted during a stay in Germany from April 1914 to December 1915, *Painting No. 4 (A Black Horse)* is part of Hartley's "Amerika" series, which he began during the summer and fall of 1914. In these paintings Hartley incorporated motifs from Native American culture in order to evoke a uniquely American spiritual aesthetic, distinct from the African and Asian sources many of his European colleagues found compelling.

The black horse, bearing the number eight on its hindquarters, occupies the physical and symbolic center of this painting. Appearing in many of Hartley's paintings from this period, the number eight held universal mystical significance for the artist and also referred specifically to the eight-pointed star he observed on royal and military insignia throughout Berlin. Hartley's incorporation of the number eight into his "Amerika" series suggests that his belief in abstract symbols was transcendently cross-cultural. The horse also appeared in Hartley's paintings of both German and Native American themes. Although the image of the horse and rider may have reflected those found in the paintings of his friend Franz Marc, it simultaneously represented the strength and grace of an animal popularly associated with Native American culture.

As in most of the "Amerika" series, in *Painting No. 4 (A Black Horse)* Hartley combined bright primary colors and simple geometric forms that extend out to the painted frame. Fish, birds, and flowering trees surround the black horse in an evocation of harmonious growth and fertility. Produced just as war was about to be declared in Europe, this painting and others from the "Amerika" series express Hartley's admiration and longing for a culture he perceived to be nobler and more peaceful.

FRANCIS PICABIA (French, 1879–1953)

Catch as Catch Can, 1913
Oil on canvas, 39⅝ x 32⅛ inches
The Louise and Walter Arensberg Collection

When Picabia first exhibited his work in the United States, at the Armory Show of 1913, the *New York Times* dubbed him "the Cuban who outcubed the Cubists," a reference to the artist's Caribbean heritage. By that time Picabia had already caught the attention of the Paris art world, having enjoyed a prodigious early success in reviving the Impressionist style of painting at the beginning of the twentieth century. The artist changed direction dramatically following his first contacts, in 1911, with Marcel Duchamp and with Guillaume Apollinaire, the poet and champion of Cubism. Abandoning his Impressionist mode, Picabia began to experiment with abstract painting, demonstrating a highly individualistic approach to Cubism characterized by vivid color harmonies. *Catch as Catch Can* dates from shortly after the Armory Show, one of an ambitious sequence of paintings inspired by his *succès de scandale* in New York.

Picabia based several of his Cubist paintings on events from his personal life, and *Catch as Catch Can* is no exception. The artist's first wife, Gabrielle, recalled that while eating in a restaurant one evening, she, Apollinaire, and Picabia became fascinated by a fearsome Chinese wrestler seated nearby. They followed the enormous man to a match of catch-as-catch-can, a form of wrestling in which usually forbidden moves such as trips and holds below the waist are allowed. Picabia commemorated the events of that night in this abstract painting. Vibrant bands of color and interlocking forms capture the explosive excitement of the bout, as the Chinese wrestler grapples with his opponent in front of a roaring crowd. The inscription at the bottom, "Edtaonisl 1913," relates to the popular Polish dancer Stacia Napierkowska, whose risqué dance routines served as the inspiration for a number of the artist's paintings. The artist's cryptic inscription mixes up the letters of the French words *étoil(e)* (star) and *dans(e)* (dance), using a process analogous to his pictorial arrangement of shattered color planes. Picabia appears to have combined the memory of the moving body of the star dancer with that of the no-holds-barred wrestling match in this tumultuous yet graceful composition.

 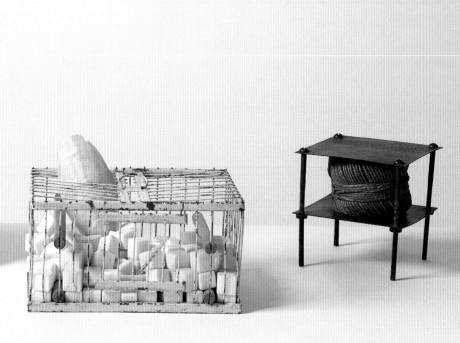

MARCEL DUCHAMP (American, born France, 1887–1968)

With Hidden Noise, 1916
Assisted Readymade: ball of twine between two brass plates, joined by four long screws, containing unknown object added by Walter Arensberg, 5 x 5 x 5⅛ inches
The Louise and Walter Arensberg Collection

Apolinère Enameled, 1916–17
Assisted Readymade: graphite on cardboard and painted tin, 9⅝ x 13⅜ inches
The Louise and Walter Arensberg Collection

Why Not Sneeze, Rose Sélavy?, 1921
Assisted Readymade: painted metal birdcage, marble cubes, porcelain dish, thermometer, and cuttlebone, 4⅞ x 8¾ x 6⅜ inches
The Louise and Walter Arensberg Collection

The commonplace objects that Duchamp chose as "Readymade" works of art epitomized the artist's belief that art should go beyond the visual and appeal to the mind as well as the senses. Duchamp began signing and giving titles to mass-produced items after he moved to New York in 1915, beginning with a snow shovel purchased in a hardware store. *With Hidden Noise* marks the transition from Duchamp's signed objects to more elaborate works, which Duchamp called "assisted Readymades." For this piece, made on Easter Day 1916, Duchamp set a ball of nautical twine between two brass plates. He then asked his friend and patron Walter Arensberg to place an unknown object inside before he clamped the Readymade shut with four long screws. The title alludes to the rattling sound the hidden object makes when shaken. Duchamp requested that Arensberg never tell him what the secret thing was, preferring to remain blissfully ignorant of his work's "content."

Another assisted Readymade, *Apolinère Enameled,* was a humorous homage to his friend the poet Guillaume Apollinaire. The tin sign, which Duchamp probably obtained from a paint store, was an advertisement for Sapolin enamel, a brand of industrial paint commonly used on radiators. The artist carefully manipulated the lettering in the commercially printed plaque, obscuring the *S* in Sapolin and adding new letters in white paint to evoke the poet's name, albeit intentionally misspelled. Duchamp also delicately shaded in pencil the reflection of the little girl's hair in the mirror.

Why Not Sneeze, Rose Sélavy? was the last Readymade Duchamp produced. The title, inscribed on the bottom of the birdcage in black adhesive tape, poses an enigmatic question in English. It is posed to, or perhaps by, Rose (later Rrose) Sélavy, the scandalous female alter ego Duchamp devised for himself (and a pun, in French, for "Eros, such is life"). The painted metal birdcage is "assisted" by the addition of 152 white marble "sugar" cubes, a mercury thermometer, a piece of cuttlebone, and a tiny porcelain dish. Its full delight comes only with use, as one is surprised by the weight of the marble, expecting the lightness of sugar lumps.

FRANCES SIMPSON STEVENS
(American, 1894–1976)

Dynamic Velocity of Interborough Rapid Transit Power Station, c. 1915
Oil and charcoal on canvas, 48⅜ x 35⅞ inches
The Louise and Walter Arensberg Collection

Dynamic Velocity of Interborough Rapid Transit Power Station holds the intriguing distinction of being the only known painting still in existence by Frances Simpson Stevens, a member of the international avant-garde early in the twentieth century. Stevens worked and exhibited in New York from 1914 until 1919, and then married a Russian aristocrat and left to live with him abroad. As Stevens's life later took different directions, her works were lost or destroyed, and eventually she died a forgotten figure in a California sanatorium.

Born in Chicago and educated in New England, Stevens enrolled in summer classes in Madrid led by the American artist Robert Henri in 1912. The following year a painting of hers was accepted for the historic Armory Show in New York. A stay in Florence in 1913–14 and Stevens's encounter with the Italian Futurist artists and writers there determined her artistic path. She quickly adopted the Futurist vocabulary, which imbued the Cubist approach to painting with a polemic extolling modern technology. A participant in Futurist exhibitions, Stevens was one of several female artists paradoxically welcomed by a group that hailed the virtues of virile aggression in painting and in life.

The Futurist credo translated readily to New York, where the cityscape of bridges and skyscrapers made it a quintessential symbol of modernity. *Dynamic Velocity* bespeaks the Futurist infatuation with technology both in its subject—the grinding turbines of a subway power station—and in its technique—bold strokes of charcoal and black oil paint that sharply attack the canvas. Its series of arcs and diagonals give the painting an effective sense of repeating motion as well as deep space, while its title adopts the Italian Futurists' preference for naming their works in relation to such values as speed and light.

MORTON LIVINGSTON SCHAMBERG
(American, 1881–1918)

Painting VIII (Mechanical Abstraction), 1916
Oil on canvas, 30⅛ x 20¼ inches
The Louise and Walter Arensberg Collection

This painting is one of a series of nine exquisitely
crafted images of individual machines that Morton
Schamberg made in Philadelphia in 1916. These cool
and austere pictures reveal the artist's appreciation of
the formal beauty of machinery and industrial manufac-
turing. They can be viewed today as an important pre-
cursor of the Precisionist aesthetic developed by
Schamberg's lifelong friend Charles Sheeler, among
others, in the 1920s. The immediate inspiration can
be found in Marcel Duchamp's precisely rendered
chocolate-grinder paintings and Francis Picabia's
schematic portraits, although Schamberg's deperson-
alized mechanical abstractions do not exhibit the sexual symbolism or cryptic humor found in the work of
his French colleagues. A more quotidian source for his
machine images came from illustrated trade cata-
logues, which Schamberg borrowed from his brother-
in-law, who manufactured ladies' cotton stockings.

Schamberg's model for *Painting VIII (Mechanical
Abstraction)* was an automated wire stitcher, a machine
used in the printing industry for binding books. Painted
in muted metallic colors, the stitching machine is comprised of a spool and curved armature holding the wire
at the top, with a drive wheel and a mechanical needle
below. In each image in the series, the artist isolated
the subject from its industrial environment and placed
it against a monochromatic background that enhances
the iconic appearance of the machinery. Schamberg's
crisp representation of a single machine, immaculately
rendered and showing all the individual working parts,
sometimes in cross-section, recalls his early training at
the University of Pennsylvania as an architect.

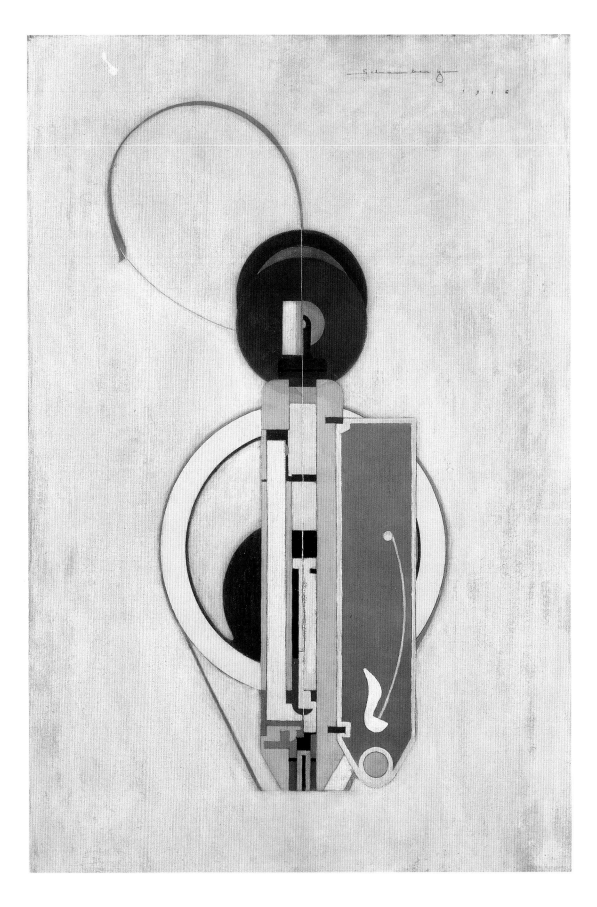

ARTHUR DOVE (American, 1880–1946)

Chinese Music, 1923
Oil and metallic paint on panel, 21 11/16 x 18 1/8 inches
The Alfred Stieglitz Collection

Dove created abstract paintings, or "extractions," as
he called them, to convey his profound response to
the rhythms and forces of the natural world. *Chinese
Music* is an early example of the artist's use of shimmering, disc-like shapes as symbols for sun, moon,
and sea. Progressively scaled to suggest gently
expansive movement, these radiating orbs are lightly
shaded with metallic silver paint and glazed translucent green. The topmost form has a serrated edge
that echoes the pale green saw-toothed form, tipped
with black, which rises from the bottom of the canvas
like a circular saw. These radial shapes intersect and
overlap with a series of dark, planar elements, suggestive of buildings, rooftops, and inverted fans; this
painting initiated a pictorial vocabulary that would sus-
tain the artist over the next two decades. The picture
was one of only three works by Dove that Stieglitz
chose to be included in the Société Anonyme's landmark International Exhibition of Modern Art, held at the
Brooklyn Museum in 1926.

The title probably comes from Arthur Jerome Eddy's
Cubists and Post-Impressionism, a survey of modern
art published in 1914, in which the author used an
analogy to Chinese music to explain the importance
of Kandinsky's nonrepresentational works: "The great
majority of people on first hearing Chinese music
exclaim, 'What a horrid din!' and turn away. A very,
very small minority, about one man in a million, say,
'True, it sounds to us like a din, but to a people of
extraordinary civilization it is music; the matter is worth
investigating.'"[†] Dove appears to have taken this public defense of abstract art as the point of departure
for a dynamic and heartfelt composition that trans-
lates the clashing harmonies of Chinese music into
visual terms. The subjective association of sound and
color, known as synesthesia, was popular within the
Stieglitz circle. Dove's interest in the notion of "visual
music" was stimulated by Kandinsky's 1912 book
Concerning the Spiritual in Art, which relates the
sounds of particular instruments to specific colors.

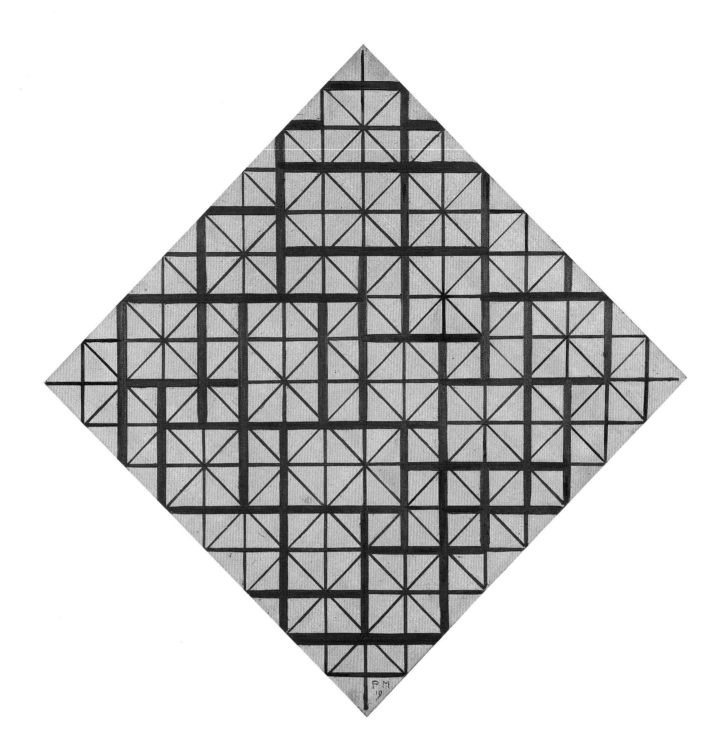

PIET MONDRIAN (Dutch, 1872–1944)

Composition with Grid 4 (Lozenge), 1919
Oil on canvas, 23⅝ x 23¹¹⁄₁₆ inches
The Louise and Walter Arensberg Collection

Mondrian is best known as the creator of perhaps the most rigorously abstract paintings of the first half of the twentieth century. His austere approach, which he called Neo-Plasticism, defined a picture plane only by vertical and horizontal lines, and by black, white, and the three primary colors. This style has become a cliché of modernism, its popular translations ranging from couture dresses by Yves Saint-Laurent to oversized beach towels. Less well known, however, is the long road Mondrian traveled to arrive at his signature idiom. The journey began in his schooling at the Royal Academy in Amsterdam and charted a course that only gradually took him from an approach based on observed nature to one of supposedly pure and universal pictorial relationships.

This painting, made when Mondrian was forty-seven, comes on the eve of his invention of Neo-Plasticism. The impact of Cubism had already taken him away from the descriptive colors and rolling contours of his early landscapes. Here Mondrian explored the visual possibilities of working with a regular grid pattern to define an entire painting. He limited his resources to linear elements in dark gray that overlay a thin white wash. Narrow diagonal lines map a network of diamonds echoing the orientation of the stretched canvas, while horizontal and vertical lines divide the diamonds into 256 triangles. The verticals and horizontals vary considerably in thickness as they span the canvas, creating the sensation of intersecting rectangular and square compartments of different shapes and sizes. The result produces an optical illusion of subtle flickering and an animated pictorial architecture that transcends its elementary means.

FERNAND LÉGER (French, 1881–1955)

The City, 1919
Oil on canvas, 91 x 117½ inches
A. E. Gallatin Collection

The staccato rhythm of Léger's *The City* produces the sensation of living in or moving through a machine-age urban environment. Visual and aural stimuli condense into a kaleidoscope of shallow, overlapping planes, signs, and fragments. The abbreviated city sights, mechanical elements, and abstract forms deliberately lack natural continuity or sequential coherence. The monumental scale of the canvas envelops the viewer like a theater backdrop, inviting us to join the mechanized figures climbing the staircase in the foreground in order to enter this bustling modern metropolis. The fragmented cityscape is illuminated by the intensity of Léger's palette—vivid hues suggesting the dazzle of modern advertising and the glare of street lighting.

The taut, geometric composition is built up with distinct areas of flat, unmodulated colors that produce depth and movement without resorting to the traditional chiaroscuro method of modeling light and shade. The scaffolding, buildings, steel structures, bridges, billboards, shopwindow mannequins in silhouette, rounded plumes of smoke, and telephone pole are rendered in primary reds, yellows, and blues contrasting with vibrant greens, purples, and grays. Passages of black and white separate the blocks of pure tones into individual compartments, with contrasts and ruptures evoking the density of the city. The pungent blacks provide graphic clarity, while the extensive use of white provides an optical light that appears to burn from within the picture. The artist has included his own initials, "F L," among the chaotic jumble of stenciled letters, recalling the colorful posters of the Place de Clichy, where Parisians are bombarded by a deluge of advertising billboards and commercial signs.

GEORGES BRAQUE (French, 1882–1963)

The Table, 1918
Oil on canvas, 52 5/16 x 29 3/4 inches
The Louise and Walter Arensberg Collection

Still life provided Braque with inexhaustible lifelong
subject matter. Like his great French predecessor
Jean-Baptiste-Siméon Chardin, he found the seemingly
limited platform of the tabletop a richly ample universe
for his pictorial explorations. But whereas eighteenth-
century artists such as Chardin attached symbolic significance to their still-life objects, Braque felt no such
obligation for a painting to harbor meaning. Nor was
he required to provide the illusion of a clear and
defined space. As direct heir to the experimentation
of Cézanne and partner of Picasso in the invention of
Cubism, Braque used the still life as a vehicle for the
development of a visual language accountable to its
own rules rather than to nature.

The Table asserts that, for Braque, these rules concerned the animation of a flat picture plane through
rhythm, texture, color, and shape. Recognizable
elements remain: a pear, grapes, a newspaper (with
the masthead "j[ourn]al"), a playing card, a rectangular
tabletop, curving feet. But echoing contours, overlapping planes, and syncopated tonalities provide the
coherence and structure that allow the composition
to stand independent of resemblance to an actual
table. *The Table* hails from Braque's first year of
work after two years of recovery from a severe head
wound suffered in World War I. In a sense, the hiatus
returned him to his roots: the new paintings exemplified the delight and virtuosity in the craft of painting
stemming from Braque's childhood as the son of a
painter-decorator, when he learned such techniques
as false wood graining, marbleizing, and lettering.
The sensuous textures and decorative surfaces—
the different wood patterns, the polka dots, the soft
letters situating us in a "[ca]fe-bar"—enliven the
picture with the distinct air of pleasure and poetry
central to Braque's celebration of painting.

JOAN MIRÓ (Spanish, 1893–1983)

Horse, Pipe, and Red Flower, 1920
Oil on canvas, 32½ x 29½ inches
Gift of Mr. and Mrs. C. Earle Miller

Horse, Pipe, and Red Flower belongs to a small number of still lifes that the Catalan artist Joan Miró painted while at home in the village of Montroig during the summer of 1920. That spring he had made his first trip to Paris, a four-month stay inspiring him with confidence and energy that bore fruit in his next paintings, the first true masterpieces of his long career. This visit to Paris initiated Miró's lifelong pattern of alternating workplaces from the French city that was the center of the artistic universe to the Catalonian countryside he dearly loved.

This joyful painting captures a moment of profound transition for the twenty-seven-year-old artist. It has the exuberant color, clamorous patterning, and chock-full composition of his earlier paintings. Miró even inserted a reference to his own landscapes of the late teens by presenting one such painting in an oval format on the wall behind the table. The bulging table, toy horse, and long clay pipe lend a Catalan flavor to the scene. But the complex configuration of the forms, the unconventional vantage point, and the background's resemblance to Cubist collage prove Miró's close attention to the avant-garde painting he saw in Paris. He focused especially on Picasso, an artist twelve years his senior whom he met during the spring of 1920. The book on the table advertises this association: it faithfully represents the small volume *Le Coq et l'arlequin,* by Jean Cocteau, illustrated with line drawings by Picasso. By audaciously incorporating Picasso's drawing in his own painting, Miró proudly announced the position he took for himself as a member of the international avant-garde.

EL (ELEAZAR) LISSITZKY (Russian, 1890–1941)

Proun 2 (Construction), 1920
Oil, paper, and metal on panel, 23$\frac{7}{16}$ x 15$\frac{11}{16}$ inches
A. E. Gallatin Collection

Lissitzky's wide-ranging innovations in painting, architecture, typography, and photography emanate from his earliest venture into abstract art, the body of works he called "Prouns," created between 1919 and 1923. Named after the Russian acronym for "Project for the Establishment of a New Art," this series of paintings, prints, and drawings was produced in the climate of utopian expectation immediately following the Russian revolution, when many artists believed in the power of art to change the world. Lissitzky did not attach his art to concrete political goals, a position that eventually brought him into conflict with his colleagues. But he was committed to the idea that society could be modernized through the transformation of perception, a vision expressed in the Prouns.

All the Prouns have in common an organization of geometric shapes dispersed as if seen from an aerial perspective. *Proun 2 (Construction),* comprised of overlapping rectangles, squares, triangles, and semicircles arranged along a variety of axes, recalls an architectural drawing or a model set in motion. Its textured materials include paper, metal, and oil paint on a wooden panel. These serve as a concrete counterpoint to the dynamic, floating spatial arrangement and refer to the realm of architectural construction, which guided the artist's conception of the Prouns. Lissitzky's interest in architecture soon led him to extend the Proun aesthetic into three dimensions. The pioneering models of exhibition design that he realized in the 1920s, a period when he lived in Berlin, were but one manifestation of the vital link he was able to forge between avant-garde artists working in Russia, Germany, France, and Holland.

MARCEL DUCHAMP (American, born France, 1887–1968)

The Bride Stripped Bare by Her Bachelors, Even (The Large Glass), 1915–23
Oil, varnish, lead foil, lead wire, and dust on two glass panels, 109¼ x 69¼ inches
Bequest of Katherine S. Dreier

Duchamp's *Large Glass* is as radical in appearance as in its intentions and implications. A work of art to be looked both through and at, neither a painting nor a sculpture, Duchamp called the *Glass* a "hilarious picture" but took it seriously enough to devote eight years to its making. He began work on his magnum opus as a twenty-seven-year-old newcomer to New York, having had it in mind since 1912. The *Glass* could not appear more different from the Readymades contemporary to it: complicated to manufacture, replete with narrative, and deeply entangled with art and science.

The *Glass* is also closely involved with words; Duchamp prepared a voluminous body of notes that articulate the narrative described by the full title of the *Glass*. He published ninety-four of these notes in individual facsimiles in 1934 in *The Green Box*, and they permit a tentative reading of the imagery of the *Glass*. As described in his notes, Duchamp's "delay in glass" chronicles the state of perpetual desire involving the bride, depicted in the upper panel, and the circle of nine uniformed bachelors arrayed in the lower. Duchamp devised an elaborate iconography to demonstrate the erotic proceedings and characterize the unfortunate actors. Every visual element of the *Glass* is the result of meticulous studies, calculations, and experiments.

In 1923 Duchamp declared the *Glass* "definitively unfinished." His decision was prophetic, as the final appearance of the work was yet to be achieved. That occurred by chance when the two panels were shattered while the *Glass* was in transit following an exhibition at the Brooklyn Museum in 1926–27. Duchamp laboriously glued it back together ten years later, securing the original glass between new panes and housing it in an aluminum frame. Occupying the spot in the Philadelphia Museum chosen for it by Duchamp a half-century ago, the *Glass* continues to generate endless speculation and inspiration for followers of its enigmatic, amusing, and irresistibly compelling tale.

HENRI MATISSE (French, 1869–1954)

Seated Nude, c. 1925
Bronze, height with base 56¾ inches
Gift of R. Sturgis and Marion B. F. Ingersoll

Matisse's paintings far outnumber his sculptures, but the interaction between his work in two dimensions and three dimensions became essential to his creations in both mediums. Not only did he paint and sculpt before the live model, but he also represented his own sculptures in his paintings and then borrowed the poses of figures he painted to derive new sculptural compositions. As the artist described it, moving back and forth between painting and sculpture allowed him to refine his ideas and condense the sensations on which his work depended: "I took up sculpture because what interested me in painting was a clarification of my ideas. . . . It was done for the purposes of organization, to put order into my feelings, and find a style to suit me. When I found it in sculpture, it helped me in my painting. It was always in view of a complete possession of my mind, a sort of hierarchy of all my sensations, that I kept working in the hope of finding an ultimate method."[†]

Seated Nude is Matisse's most ambitious sculpture of the 1920s. It is part of the matrix of drawings, lithographs, and paintings that Matisse made of the model Henriette Darricarrère posed with raised arms and with her left foot hooked casually behind her knee. A crystallization of the artist's successive reactions to the model's relaxed pose, the sculpture transforms her body into a tautly structured abstract composition. Even more than in his earlier sculptures, Matisse treated the human figure as an arrangement of discrete parts, allowing himself great liberty to consider separately the variety of possible views in three dimensions. Each surface of the model's elongated torso, diminutive head, and weighty limbs is articulated as a succession of planes carving space. The seams and cuts on the surface of the sculpture, evidence of the artist's working process, both absorb light and reflect it, adding complexity to the way the sculpture engages its surrounding space. Dramatically cantilevered from its small base, *Seated Nude* projects a confident balance of its parts, subordinating anatomical reality to a powerful sculptural whole.

PABLO PICASSO (Spanish, 1881–1973)

Three Musicians, 1921
Oil on canvas, 80½ x 74⅛ inches
A. E. Gallatin Collection

Picasso painted *Three Musicians* in the garage of the villa he rented at Fontainebleau for the summer of 1921. This solemnly majestic oil painting, with its flat, patterned shapes echoing the cut and pasted papers of his collages, provides a grand summation of the artist's decade-long exploration of Synthetic Cubism. The three masked figures, with their sinister smiles and humorous false mustaches, are rendered in flat, overlapping planes that give them an intangible, paper-

thin quality, which increases the strange, otherworldly atmosphere of this Cubist concert. Like actors on a stage, the musicians are arranged frontally in a shallow, boxlike space. Harlequin holds a violin and bow, Pierrot plays a clarinet (or recorder) above a sheet of music unfolded on the table, and a Franciscan friar in a homespun habit with a rope for his belt holds an accordion.

The appearance of costumed figures, derived from Italian popular theater and carnival traditions, also relates to Picasso's collaboration, beginning in 1917, with the Russian ballet. In the year before he painted *Three Musicians,* Picasso had designed costumes for Sergei Diaghilev's ballet *Pulcinella,* which had

choreography based directly on commedia dell'arte types. The painting has also been interpreted as a symbolic and nostalgic elegy to Picasso's poet friends or his own lost bohemian youth.[†] According to this biographical reading, the mysterious triumvirate commemorates the recently deceased Guillaume Apollinaire, in the form of Pierrot, with the poet Max Jacob as the friar and Picasso himself as Harlequin, the sad-clown figure with whom he had identified in his earlier work. Picasso refused to part with the work for many years, before finally letting A. E. Gallatin acquire it for his Gallery of Living Art in New York in 1936. Gallatin was able to purchase the painting just before the Museum of Modern Art, which later bought another version of the subject.

KURT SCHWITTERS (German, 1887–1948)

Merz Construction, c. 1921
Painted wood, wire mesh, cardboard, and paper,
15 x 8¼ inches
A. E. Gallatin Collection

This engaging object appears to be a cross between
a Cubist collage, a wall clock, and a kindergarten
project. It hangs on the wall with an undeniable dignity
that transforms its humble scraps of wood, metal,
cardboard, and wire into the proud raw material of abstract art. The formal structure of Schwitters's Merz
compositions derives from his subtle layering of texture
and color and careful syncopation of shapes and planar
segments. A persuasive sense of mechanical potential
arises from the interrelated workings of its components: the gray knob with its tip painted red, the gear-
like discs, and the marvelous wedge in the lower right
ready to kick into action. The bright blue, pink, yellow,
and red proclaim its maker's delight in the creative
potential of society's discards and leftovers.

This construction is a classic example of Merz, an art
form invented by and unique to Schwitters. It came to
include not only collage and assemblage but poetry,
graphic design, and sculpture. Schwitters adopted the
name from a 1918 assemblage that included the typo-
graphic fragment "merz," excerpted from a poster for
the "Commerz und Privatbank." He later explained that
Merz "denotes essentially the combination of all con-
ceivable materials for artistic purposes. . . . The artist
creates through the choice, distribution and metamor-
phosis of the materials."[†] Schwitters's nature was that
of an inveterate forager and he had a genuine fondness for all sorts of odds and ends. But he also had
an ideological commitment to Merz: a desire to erase
the opposition between the realm of art and the ordinariness of daily life. Like other artists associated with
the Dada movement, Schwitters was often mistakenly
condemned as an attacker of art. In reality he offered
it fresh life, inventing a world of new materials and
formats that would inspire future artists ranging from
Robert Rauschenberg to Gabriel Orozco.

PAUL KLEE (Swiss, 1879–1940)

Fish Magic, 1925
Oil and watercolor on canvas with muslin on panel,
30 ⅜ x 38 ¾ inches
The Louise and Walter Arensberg Collection

Fish Magic is set squarely in the tradition of German
Romanticism, with its blend of fantasy and natural
empiricism, of poetry and pragmatics. That Romantic
heritage led Klee to become one of modern art's
greatest fantasists as well as one of its major theo-
rists, especially in the field of color. His art is most
beloved for its unending reserve of charming whimsy,
inevitably bringing smiles to the least likely faces. Yet,
during his decade as an instructor at the Bauhaus, the
renowned German art and design school, Klee produced volumes of writings in which technical advice
rises to the level of the philosophical. These two
seemingly opposite poles of Klee's nature joined
forces to inspire his unending experimentation with
mediums and materials. Klee's technical knowledge
and exactitude allowed the magician in him to conjure
visions that delight and amaze.

In *Fish Magic,* made in the middle of Klee's period at
the Bauhaus, the aquatic, celestial, and earthly realms
intermingle. They do so in an inky black atmosphere of
indeterminate scale and scope, where fish and flora
float among human beings or clock towers. The delicate black surface that washes over the entire canvas
covers an underlayer dense with multicolored

pigments. Klee scraped and sanded the black paint to
reveal mysterious specks and passages of glowing
color underneath, a sophisticated version of the
games children play with wax crayons. But Klee inge-
niously conceived a device to imply that more mysteries await to be unveiled. The painting is, in fact, a
collage, with a central square of muslin glued on top
of the larger rectangular canvas surface. A long diagonal line reaching to the top of the clock tower from the
side is poised to whisk off this subtle curtain. For
Klee, art was always theater and, like all his paintings,
this one provides a promise of more acts to follow.

JEAN ARP (French, born Switzerland, 1887–1966)

Configuration with Two Dangerous Points, 1930
Painted wood, 27⅝ x 33⅜ inches
A. E. Gallatin Collection

Marcel Duchamp once credited Jean Arp with showing "the importance of a smile to combat the sophistic theories of the moment."† The Swiss-born artist, who began his career in Zurich during World War I as a member of Dada, indeed reacted against the pessimism of the time by incorporating lighthearted innocence into his own iconoclastic art. Throughout his life, Arp, who lived and worked in Switzerland, France,

and Germany, refused to be identified with any single philosophy of art or any single medium. However, the painted wood reliefs he first made in Zurich, a group of brightly colored, layered, plantlike forms resembling children's puzzles, were a genre he returned to periodically during his career. Infatuated with the notion of chance as a natural, animating force, he exploited the possibilities of the random and the uncanny in his "constellations," a group of primarily black-and-white relief sculptures he made in Paris in the 1930s.

One of the earliest of the group, *Configuration with Two Dangerous Points* shows the formal elegance Arp achieved in works that took inspiration from

organic processes and shapes found in nature to evolve a more austere abstract aesthetic. The sculpture is composed of four white amoeboid shapes, one punctured with two holes, affixed to a surface painted with two similar black biomorphic forms. Its format is reminiscent of a gameboard arrayed with playing pieces. The artist's devotion to models of play to generate art and poetry extends to the humorously provocative title, which does not describe what we see and purposely contradicts the sensibility projected by this harmonious composition of rounded, rhyming, organic forms.

JOAN MIRÓ (Spanish, 1893–1983)

Dog Barking at the Moon, 1926
Oil on canvas, 28¾ x 36¼ inches
A. E. Gallatin Collection

From a seemingly quotidian subject—a dog barking at the moon—Miró crafted a painting that is fanciful, nostalgic, and replete with metaphysical yearning. As is true of many of the works he painted when he was living intermittently in France and in his native Spain, this work registers memories of the Catalonian landscape, which remained the emotional center of his painting and the source of his imagery for much

of his life. Created shortly after Miró first included words in his art in what he called "painting-poems," its genesis lies in a sketch by the artist showing the moon rejecting a dog's plaintive yelps, saying in Catalan, "You know, I don't give a damn." The import of these words, crossed out in the drawing and then excluded from the painting, nonetheless lingers in the vacant space between the few pictorial elements that compose this stark yet whimsical image of frustrated longing.

Against the simple background, the artist has painted a dog, ladder, moon, and bird. These brightly painted signs arrayed across the field have the quality of words

on a blank page. The ladder receding into the sky lends a sense of deep, vacant space to this scene of nocturnal isolation. Stretching across the meandering horizon line and into the distance, this frequently repeated element of the artist's personal iconography suggests the dream of escape or else a poignant desire for connection between the terrestrial and the cosmic. The remarkable combination of earthiness, mysticism, and humor with a rigorous formal imagination marked Miró's successful merging of international artistic preoccupations with an emphatically regional outlook to arrive at his distinctively personal and deeply poetic sensibility.

GEORGE BIDDLE (American, 1885–1973)

Whoopee at Sloppy Joe's, 1933
Oil on canvas, 40½ x 40⅜ inches
Gift of the artist

Whoopee at Sloppy Joe's belongs to George Biddle's series of paintings about high society life under Prohibition. A portrayal both affectionate and satirical, it is rendered, one feels, by a seasoned veteran of many such evenings. Born in Philadelphia, Biddle had traded Harvard Law School training for an artistic career. Extensive world travel had introduced him to European contemporaries as well as to ancient cultures, all of which he filtered into a personal style marked by linear elegance and tonal delicacy. Here, muted shades of green, brown, gray, and silvery whites are applied in powdery oil paint that suggests tempera. Biddle's sharp eye precisely captures the inhabitants of this decadent milieu: sad-eyed, seen-everything bartenders; a predatory Lothario with nervous female prey; rouge-cheeked, red-lipped, aging gentlemen; a sagging, dejected lone drinker. The artist's decision to portray the corner of the bar sets up a diagonal background that renders everything askew, simulating for the viewer a state of inebriated vision.

Shortly after Biddle finished the series of speakeasy paintings, his subject of high society gave way to imagery more characteristic of the Depression years and expressive of what Biddle called "spiritual nobility." He was instrumental in founding the Works Progress Administration (WPA), and he designed and painted the fresco murals that fill the lobby of the Justice Department building in Washington, D.C., inspired by examples he had recently studied in Mexico and Italy. These and other murals, like his many portraits (four of which are in this Museum's collection), reveal Biddle's acute powers of observation and characterization, whether applied to entertaining, intimate, or inspirational ends.

FLORINE STETTHEIMER (American, 1871–1948)

Spring Sale at Bendel's, 1921
Oil on canvas, 50 x 40 inches
Gift of Miss Ettie Stettheimer

Florine Stettheimer offers her audience a humorous
look into the chaotic world of high fashion at bargain
prices. Demonstrating Stettheimer's fondness for
clever critiques of her urban milieu, the painting
features her typical jewel-like palette of bright reds,
oranges, yellows, greens, and pinks. Along with her
two sisters and their mother, Florine Stettheimer
presided over one of Manhattan's premier intellectual
salons during the teens and twenties, with guests
including such artists and writers as Marcel Duchamp,
Charles Demuth, Alfred Stieglitz, and Carl Van Vechten.
Beginning in the years between 1910 and 1920,
Stettheimer produced many portraits of her friends
and family, depicting the sociable interactions of the
American avant-garde at picnics and cocktail parties.
Spring Sale at Bendel's introduces the playful
commentary on capitalist enterprise that Stettheimer
would most fully explore in her "Cathedral" series,
such as *Cathedrals of Fifth Avenue* (1931)
and *Cathedrals of Wall Street* (1939).

Here Stettheimer wittily portrays the indecorous
behavior of her own upper class. The opulent red
draperies part to reveal an inner sanctum of privilege
and luxury. New York's elite leap across tables to
snatch up luxurious fabrics, twisting and preening to
assess the glamorous effects of the merchandise.
The sensation of witnessing the nearly scandalous
pleasure of women shopping is heightened by the
occasional glimpse of a garter here and there and
the presence of only two men in the entire composition. The frenzy of attenuated women scattered
across the canvas is tempered by the figure of
the calm sales manager at the foot of the grand
staircase, ringleader of this retail circus. In a final
gesture of amusing extravagance, Stettheimer signed
the painting by including her initials as a mono-
grammed sweater on the Pekingese dog politely
waiting in the corner.

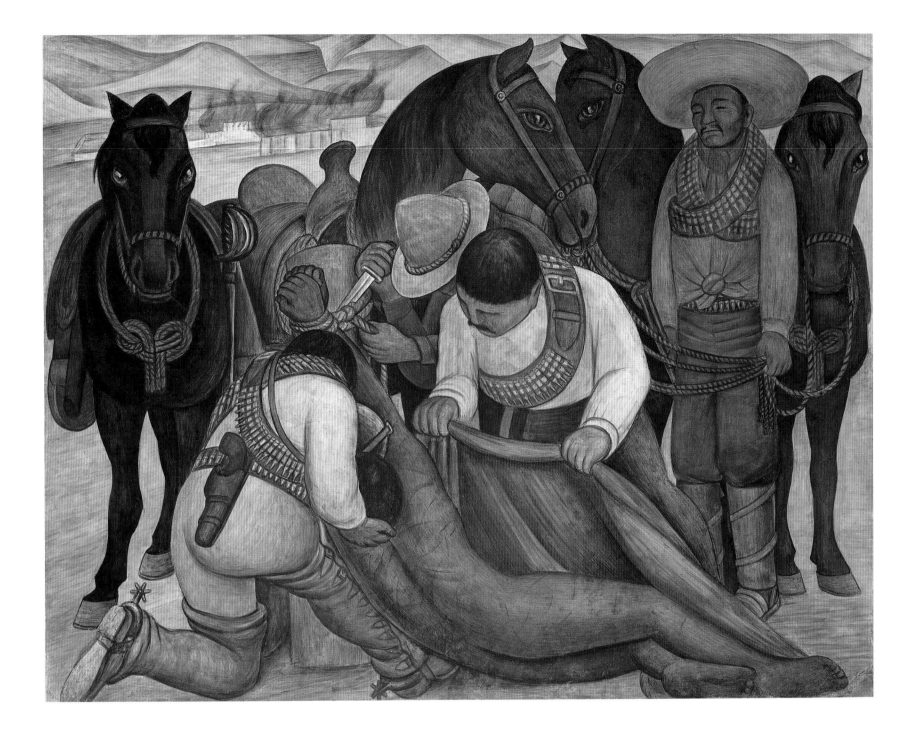

JOSÉ DIEGO MARIA RIVERA (Mexican, 1886–1957)

Sugar Cane, 1931
Fresco, 57⅛ x 94⅛ inches
Gift of Mr. and Mrs. Herbert Cameron Morris

Liberation of the Peon, 1931
Fresco, 73 x 94¼ inches
Gift of Mr. and Mrs. Herbert Cameron Morris

These two portable fresco panels were painted by Rivera in New York on the occasion of his exhibition at the Museum of Modern Art, which opened in December 1931 and later traveled to Philadelphia. A leading figure in the Mexican mural movement, Rivera sought to illustrate Mexican history, before and after the revolution of 1911–17, in a direct and straightforward way that could be understood by the masses. To achieve this aim, the muralists had revived the Italian Renaissance fresco tradition of applying pigments ground in water to a moist lime plaster wall surface. Rivera wanted the North American public to see the art form for which he was most famous, and since his murals were permanently situated on the walls of public buildings in Mexico, he decided to paint a series of movable frescoes. The artist was given a spacious studio in the Museum of Modern Art building and completed eight fresco panels during his stay there. *Sugar Cane* is based on one of the artist's murals at the Palace of Cortés in Cuernavaca, completed in 1930, and *Liberation of the Peon* is adapted from a mural cycle in the Ministry of Public Education building in Mexico City, painted in 1923.

Sugar Cane depicts the harsh reality of life for ordinary Mexicans in the southern state of Morelos before Emiliano Zapata led the agrarian revolution there in 1911. Rivera contrasts the languid pose of the sugar plantation owner, indolently stretched in his hammock in the background, with the backbreaking work carried out by the peasant laborers, watched over by a menacing foreman on horseback. *Liberation of the Peon* symbolizes the struggle to free peasants from this life of unremitting toil, as four revolutionary soldiers release a man who has been severely flogged and left for dead. Rivera designed his composition to echo scenes of Christ's descent from the cross and the Lamentation. The soldiers attend the naked, lacerated peon and prepare to wrap him in a red robe, while the burning hacienda in the background heralds the end of colonial exploitation.

JOAQUÍN TORRES-GARCÍA (Uruguayan, 1874–1949)

Composition, 1929
Oil on burlap, 32 x 39 7/16 inches
A. E. Gallatin Collection

Torres-García painted *Composition* in the same year he met Mondrian in Paris. The artist's exposure to Mondrian's powerful, abstract canvases had an immediate impact upon his work, which had previously consisted of a figurative style inspired by African and pre-Columbian art. In this painting, Torres-García retained the gridded structure of Mondrian's flat,

geometric paintings but enlivened each compartmentalized rectangle with a superimposed figurative motif. The schematic imagery embedded in the creamy beige ground includes a fish, a ladder, several clocks, a man and a woman, architectural features, and what looks like a steam locomotive, all delicately shaded with pink, blue, and yellow bars to suggest a shallow relief. The letters "EXPR" (perhaps short for "express," given the visual suggestion of the train) recall the collage fragments of newspaper lettering in Cubist compositions.

Torres-García saw the integration of symbol and grid as a humanistic response to Mondrian's aesthetic. He

set out to develop a personal system of signs drawn from a wide range of sources, including indigenous Inca masonry and Peruvian textiles, architecture, and ceramics, so that his paintings could be read as a kind of pictograph or hieroglyphic text. *Composition* is one of the earliest known examples of "Universal Constructivism," as the artist called this style of painting, defined by him in an essay published in 1930 in the first issue of the Parisian magazine *Cercle et Carré* ("Circle and Square"): "a work of art must not represent nature but exist as the concrete embodiment of an idea. It must be self-contained, defined by its own order and inner rhythms."[†]

RENÉ MAGRITTE (Belgian, 1898–1967)

The Six Elements, 1929
Oil on canvas, 28¾ x 39⁵⁄₁₆ inches
The Louise and Walter Arensberg Collection

Magritte developed his art from the troubling uncertainties produced by strange juxtapositions and distortions of commonplace objects and settings. His style of painting in a smooth, illusionistic manner more commonly associated with academic or popular art than with modernist experimentation was an essential tool in the artist's lifelong project of disturbing existing assumptions about the rationality of reality and its perception by the eyes and mind. In *The Six Elements,* he

relied on this direct style of representation to depict a multipaneled picture-within-a-picture showing six components: flames, a female torso, a forest, the facade of a house, a sky with clouds, and a curtain made of lead and sleigh bells, one of his favorite enigmatic images. Magritte's title calls to mind the classic formulation of the basic elements of the universe—air, water, fire, and earth—although the links between these and his own set are elusive, presenting teasing riddles for the viewer.

Each of the elements enclosed in the framed compartments assumes a quality of isolation as if it were a discrete thought or a word. Yet the image, which seems as easily toppled as a theater set, calls into

question the notion that reality can be divided into parts and subjected to rational analyses. Reused and transformed by the artist in later paintings, these same "six elements" became central to the self-contained world of Magritte's art. Painted at the end of a three-year stay in Paris when Magritte was immersed in Surrealist circles, *The Six Elements* exemplifies the artist's ability to lure the viewer into questioning the relationship between language and images and searching for meaning behind and beyond his flat and seemingly intractable paintings.

JAMES ENSOR (Belgian, 1860–1949)

Self-Portrait with Masks, 1937
Oil on canvas, 12¼ x 9⅝ inches
The Louis E. Stern Collection

Ensor painted *Self-Portrait with Masks* when he was
seventy-seven years old and at the height of his fame.
The famously reclusive painter, who frequently used
masks in his caustic satires of Belgian society,
religion, and politics, pokes fun at himself and at his
artistic status in this small painting. Known for being a
stay-at-home curmudgeon who worked for much of his
life in the attic studio of his parents' seaside home,
Ensor must have been amused by his success in the
society that had harshly rejected him in the late 1880s,
when his best-known painting, *The Entry of Christ into
Brussels in 1889,* was refused by the Brussels avant-
garde Salon. He later described this event as a humili-
ating rejection that propelled a deep retreat: "Hounded
by those on my trail, I joyfully took refuge in the solitary land of fools where the mask, with its violence, its
brightness and brilliance, reigns supreme. The mask
meant to me freshness of colour, extravagant decoration, wild generous gestures, strident expressions,
exquisite turbulence."[†]

The artist shows himself standing before a canvas,
confronted by four Chinese masks of a type used in
the local carnival in his native Ostend and also sold in
his mother's seaside tourist shop on the ground floor
of the family home. An avid collector of these objects,
Ensor had earlier used them to make macabre self-
portraits that often included skulls. In contrast, this
benign image shows the artist well dressed and posed
before the easel with his studio props near at hand.
Dressed in a bowler hat, elegant tie, and spectacles,
brandishing a paint-dotted palette and standing
against the bright red backdrop, Ensor looks both frail
and mischievous. The masks, brought to life by his
brush, are lighthearted presences but also taunting
alter-egos of the artist that complicate his proud pose
as the well-heeled gentleman-painter in his studio.

GEORGES ROUAULT (French, 1871–1958)

Pierrot with a Rose, c. 1936
Oil on paper, 36½ x 24⁵⁄₁₆ inches
The Samuel S. White 3rd and Vera White Collection

Throughout his career, Rouault pursued a solitary
artistic path outside the mainstream of the Parisian
avant-garde. As a devoted convert to Catholicism
in his twenties, he committed himself to figurative
painting directed to religious purposes. His technical
virtuosity and innovation were anything but traditional,
however. Although *Pierrot with a Rose* is painted on
paper rather than canvas, the oil is vigorously built
up in many layers, accumulating in thick patches and
long slashing strokes. Rouault exploited the application
of thick layers of paint to impart a translucent glow
to the colorful forms outlined in black, an effect hark-
ing back to his early training in making stained glass.
Its lyrical mood and the device of painting a brightly
patterned frame within the composition itself exemplify
the decorative pleasure that came only at this late
point in Rouault's career.

Pierrot's pictures have a rich history in the French tradition. In the pantomime theater, the mute clown figure
Pierrot always suffers an unhappy fate. As such, he
belongs to a colorful population of outcast figures—
beggars, prostitutes, gypsies—popular with nineteenth-
century Romantic painters. The allure was that of
identification: the Romantic artist felt himself misunder-
stood and even reviled and thus associated himself
with other figures on the margins of society. Knit into
this web of associations is the figure of Christ, the
archetypal sacrificial victim. Rouault, in portraying this
Pierrot with a red rose, a traditional symbol of Christ's
blood, made the Christian connection explicit, com-
pleting a triangle linking the identities of sad clown,
neglected artist, and holy martyr. This loving profile of
Pierrot gains power from its unstated function as a
symbolic self-portrait.

HORACE PIPPIN (American, 1888–1946)

The End of the War: Starting Home, 1930–33
Oil on canvas, 26 x 30¹/₁₆ inches
Gift of Robert Carlen

Self-taught artist Horace Pippin started working on this painting of a World War I theme nearly fifteen years after he returned to the United States from serving in France. Wounded and paralyzed in his right arm while fighting as a member of one of four African American regiments to see combat, Pippin had turned to painting to help his process of recovery. But it was not long before he went from the obscurity of his home in Chester, Pennsylvania, to wider fame. He developed a circle of devoted collectors including the controversial Philadelphian Dr. Albert C. Barnes. The untutored quality of his pictures was celebrated for its affinity with the concerns of modern artists in the 1930s, and four of his paintings were shown at the Museum of Modern Art, New York, in the 1938 exhibition "Masters of Popular Painting."

The End of the War: Starting Home reflects the artist's traumatic wartime experiences, events he later said "brought out all the art in me."[†] This archetypal image of combat, fear, and surrender condenses tragic and terrifying episodes he had documented with drawings and accounts in his wartime journals. At its center a German soldier with raised arms is confronted by a bayonet-bearing soldier. The foreground presents other dramas: a lone soldier falls, wounded, amid numerous one-on-one confrontations while several soldiers seek safety in the trenches and forest from the threat of hidden enemy troops and barbed wire. By contrast, the vast scale of mechanized modern warfare is emphasized in the images of crashing, burning planes and multiple bombings along the distant horizon. The surface of the picture is so densely built up that it has taken on the qualities of three-dimensional relief. The artist's hand-carved frame, which shows French, British, and German weaponry and helmets, heightens the poignancy of Pippin's depiction of the human dimension of war.

CHARLES SHEELER (American, 1883–1965)

Cactus, 1931
Oil on canvas, 45⅛ x 30¹/₁₆ inches
The Louise and Walter Arensberg Collection

One of many artists who sought to capture the spirit
of modern technology in the first half of the twentieth
century, Sheeler took up such themes as machinery,
rural architecture, and industrial landscapes. Adopting
a clear, linear painting style, Sheeler's work epitomizes
the movement in American art that has come to be
known as Precisionism.

Sheeler was also a commercial photographer, and
Cactus is one of a small group of paintings in which
he depicted the interior of his photography studio in
Manhattan. It is, in fact, based on a photographic still
life Sheeler had recently produced. At first glance,
the painting itself suggests a photograph in its dominant palette of grays, blacks, and whites, and it refers
overtly to the apparatus of commercial photography
with the presence of two large studio lamps hovering
near the central plant. Neither of these lamps provides
a light source for the image, and the one on the right
is shown limply unplugged; instead, light floods in from
an unknown source to the left of the composition.

The large green cactus, sitting on the shiny tabletop,
anchors this triangle of mechanical forms. Sheeler
uses the cactus both to introduce a solid burst of color
and to provide an organic counterpoint to the rounded
form of the large, unlit bulb. At this time, the cactus
was often viewed as a botanical embodiment of the
modern, streamlined aesthetic, and Sheeler surely
also had this in mind when he chose his subject. The
photographic version of this still life reveals that the
cactus had large spiny barbs, which Sheeler deleted
in the painted version of this arrangement.

PIET MONDRIAN (Dutch, 1872–1944)

Composition, 1936
Oil on canvas, 28¾ x 26¹/₁₆ inches
The Louise and Walter Arensberg Collection

Mondrian passionately believed in art as the expression of pure and universal form. The liberation of color and line from the duties of naturalistic representation, he insisted, allowed for the fullest and most direct demonstration of art's essence. The best defense for Mondrian's theories is his own achievement as a painter. Relying on starkly limited means, his paintings are individually captivating; collectively, they tell a story with dramatic twists and turns.

Composition stems from a time when Mondrian's art had entered a phase of rhythmic animation that would govern his work for the rest of his life. His vocabulary—planes of white or primary colors and black lines—remains what it was since 1920. But structural innovations create a radically new mood. In Mondrian's classically calm compositions of the 1920s, independent black lines separate the surface into discrete planes of color or white. Here, however, Mondrian employed lines running across the canvas, parallel to each other at varying intervals. As a result, the lines divide the canvas so that they no longer read as boundaries but engage equally with the planes as actors on the painting's surface. The lines possess multiple and simultaneous identities,

partnering with different mates and viewable in different segments. No one particular rectangle asserts itself as exclusive or definitive, as each belongs to a network of overlapping and intersecting possibilities that never come to rest.

Mondrian had a predominantly ascetic temperament, but his last decade of work reflects the part of him that loved to foxtrot and listen to jazz. While it was only the final paintings of his life that he would dare to call "boogie-woogies," paintings such as this reveal the excitement of having become gloriously fluent in a language of one's own invention.

HENRY MOORE (English, 1898–1986)

Two Forms, 1936
Hornton stone, 41½ x 31 x 15 inches
Gift of Mrs. H. Gates Lloyd

Henry Moore rejected the classical ideal derived from the art of ancient Greece in favor of the raw energy and formal vigor of the art of prehistoric and non-Western cultures, in particular the pre-Columbian, Egyptian, and African art he admired in the British Museum, London. In his early sculpture, Moore worked primarily in stone, for which he had an innate sensitivity, and helped to revive in Britain the long-lost tradition of direct carving. These totemic figures were carved out of two large blocks of Hornton stone, an indigenous limestone with a brownish green tint used extensively in English churches and cathedrals. The back of one of the figures has a beautiful, rippled pattern caused by the flow of river water over the stone, which Moore left untouched in order to contrast the rough texture of the natural grooves with the smooth surface of his own carving.

Moore created *Two Forms* in the same year he helped to organize the important International Surrealist Exhibition in London. The abbreviated anatomical markings and underlying eroticism of the two figures are closely related to the work of the Surrealist artists Joan Miró and Alberto Giacometti. Moore carved the highly polished blocks with schematic incisions that mysteriously hint at body parts—ribs, nipples, eyes, and orifices—without specifically indicating a male or female gender.

The iconic presence and raw energy of these monolithic forms also evoke the giant standing stones found at Stonehenge and other sites in Britain, giving them a timeless quality despite their apparent modernity.

SALVADOR DALI (Spanish, 1904–1989)

***Soft Construction with Boiled Beans
(Premonition of Civil War),*** 1936
Oil on canvas, 39¹⁵⁄₁₆ x 39⅜ inches
The Louise and Walter Arensberg Collection

With its flair for detail as gruesome as it is meticulous,
Salvador Dali's Surrealist style might well have been
invented for the depiction of the unique horrors of the
1930s and 1940s in Europe. This painting, however,
is one of only a few in which Dali turned his attention
to the political moment. Like the mural-sized painting
Guernica by Pablo Picasso, painted one year later,
it cries out against the Spanish Civil War begun by
Francisco Franco's nationalist insurrection against the
democratic government of the Spanish republic. Over
the decades, both *Soft Construction* and *Guernica*
have come to serve as universal icons decrying
human hatred and destruction.

Dali's own words, as singular as his pictorial language,
best describe the mood of this overwrought picture:
"a vast human body breaking out into monstrous ex-
crescences of arms and legs tearing at one another
in a delirium of autostrangulation."† Dali's fellow Surrealists reveled in the desecration of the human body,
whether in painting, sculpture, or photography, but
none had yet descended to such depths of tortuous
anatomy. The ecstatic grimace, the taut neck muscles,
the elasticized torso, and the petrifying fingers and
toes all conspire to create a vision of disgusting
fascination. So persuasive is the construction's awful
presence that it appears to be an authentic natural
phenomenon, an eighth wonder of the world, rather
than merely a human figure or an imagined apparition.
With the limp phallic form draped over the truncated
hip, Dali deployed his signature device of "soft" form,
and the scattered beans of the title exemplify the
bizarre incongruities of scale he used to conjure the
workings of the unconscious mind. Dali saluted Sig-
mund Freud, whose work inspired him to embrace
his nightmarish visions, with a tiny portrait inspecting
the curling hand at the lower left.

MAN RAY (American, 1890–1976)

Le Beau Temps, 1939
Oil on canvas, 82¾ x 78¾ inches
Promised gift of Sidney and Caroline Kimmel

Man Ray painted *Le Beau Temps* just before the outbreak of World War II, and its disturbing imagery and bitterly ironic title reflect his anxiety about the impending conflict. The brightly colored composition was inspired by a series of haunting nightmares, including one involving mythological beasts locked in combat on the roof of his house in Saint-Germain-en-Laye, a suburb of Paris. It also contains a fascinating compendium of several of Man Ray's most famous images, including the two small stones tied with string that he had earlier photographed in close-up and the upturned billiard table used in a painting from the previous year.

A strange door divides the painting into two distinct sections—alluding perhaps to day and night or reality and dream. Blood trickles from the keyhole of the door and gathers in a pool on the floor. A robotlike harlequin hesitates on the verge of opening this door beyond which a female figure with a conical head and hourglass-shaped torso supporting a colorful skirt awaits him. The head of the harlequin is illuminated by a burning candle covered by a lampshade, evoking André Breton's description of Man Ray as "the man with the magic lantern head,"[†] a reference to his achievements as a photographer. The garden is protected by a decaying stone wall breached by a cannon shot. On the far side of the bloody threshold, two shadowy lovers embrace in the artist's studio, while above them a bull-like animal sinks its teeth into a reptile's throat with such ferocity that it seems engaged in not only devouring the beast but also copulating with it.

HENRI MATISSE (French, 1869–1954)

Woman in Blue, 1937
Oil on canvas, 36½ x 29 inches
Gift of Mrs. John Wintersteen

Like many of the portraits Matisse painted in the late 1930s, this work focuses on a dramatic costume rather than the personality of the sitter, whose features have been flattened and simplified with no interior modeling. The artist considered *Woman in Blue* his best picture of 1937, and, indeed, the simplicity of the composition is striking, with its palette restricted to red, yellow, blue, black, and white. A casual harmony exists among the many billowing curves of the model's dress, the background grids, and the drawings behind her on the wall. To articulate the background and the sleeves of the dress, Matisse scraped linear patterns into the wet ground with the hard end of his brush, a technique that he had first used in the portrait of Mademoiselle Landsberg. Ten photographs taken over the three months that Matisse worked on the picture (now in the Museum archives) prove that the work underwent many variations during the course of its making. The earliest version of the picture shows a comparatively naturalistic composition, full of detail and depth, of a woman leaning to her side. Only gradually did the final state evolve, with its flat picture plane, inexpressive portrayal, and boldly exaggerated right hand encircled with beads.

The model for *Woman in Blue* was Lydia Delectorskaya, a beautiful young Russian émigrée who worked for Matisse during the last twenty years of his life. The sumptuous violet-blue dress was one that Lydia herself made out of fabric that Matisse bought in Paris. The resulting concoction, which appears in several paintings of this period, was intended to be worn only in the studio and was held together by loose stitches and pins. Matisse's lifelong love of fabric and his expertise at capturing its colors, textures, and folds might be traced back to his childhood in Bohain-en-Vermandois, an industrial town in northeastern France, which was at that time an important center for the textile industry.

PABLO PICASSO (Spanish, 1881–1973)

Man with a Lamb, 1943–44
Bronze, height 79½ inches
Gift of R. Sturgis and Marion B. F. Ingersoll

From the pressure and isolation of living in German-occupied Paris during World War II, Picasso created art that was more self-conscious in its connection to the past and overtly concerned with art historical tradition. The fractured language of Cubism took on the expressiveness of medieval sculpture in his depictions of ravaged bodies, while he chose traditional memento mori objects such as skulls and candles for his still-life paintings. In his three-dimensional work, the inventor of assemblage returned to figurative sculpture and to modeling in plaster.

His most important sculpture from this period, the majestic and monumental *Man with a Lamb* originated in an etching Picasso made in 1942 on Bastille Day, July 14, of a man carrying a bouquet of flowers. In dozens of drawings the artist transformed the tranquil flowers into an agitated animal in the man's arms, making an image that recalls early Christian depictions of the Good Shepherd. Picasso emphasized the craning of the lamb's neck and the effort of the man to subdue the creature by holding its legs, preserving these motifs when he created the sculpture in clay in February or March 1943.

The tense struggle and physical energy captured by the drawings are internalized in *Man with a Lamb,* which projects a solemn and introspective quietude. The lamb, with its mouth open and one leg dangling, becomes an oversized burden in the arms of the standing man, seemingly stoic in the exertion of strength required to hold the animal. The surface is nervous and visually active, recording the construction of the sculpture piece by piece from damp clay. The spirit of this initial process is retained in the bronze version, which was cast after the liberation of Paris. Picasso's depiction of sacrifice and suffering, which he described as an expression of universal emotion, takes on heightened significance in light of the worldwide war that was being fought when he created it.

WILLEM DE KOONING (American, born Netherlands, 1904–1997)

Seated Woman, c. 1940
Oil and charcoal on Masonite, 54 1/16 x 36 inches
The Albert M. Greenfield and Elizabeth M.
Greenfield Collection

This composition is an early work from de Kooning's long sequence of paintings of women that culminated in one of the most aggressive revisions of the female figure in the art of the twentieth century. The three-quarter-length *Seated Woman* began as a study for a commissioned portrait that the artist never completed. Instead, de Kooning used the portrait as a vehicle to explore his ongoing interest in amalgamating figurative subjects with the pictorial concerns of abstraction. The beautiful female that de Kooning assembled and disassembled recalls the coolly sensuous women painted by the nineteenth-century French artist Jean-Auguste-Dominique Ingres, with their tightly fitted bodices, delicate features, and fineness of line. However, the painting's willful anatomical distortions and shifting perspectives are unquestionably related to the recent paintings of the European avant-garde.

De Kooning's struggle to redefine the female form is presented explicitly in the painted outlines and charcoal underdrawing and overdrawing that emphasize the artist's rearrangements, particularly of arms and legs. The left arm, for example, is barely hinged to the body and hangs loose, as if pulled out of its socket. The ghostlike pentimenti retain the evidence of previous incarnations of the work and reflect de Kooning's practice of sandpapering his paintings when they were dry to approximate the polished surfaces of Old Master portraits. The high-keyed pinks, blues, purples, reds, aquamarines, and oranges comprise an acidic palette typical of the artist's work of this time, when he used intense colors to define both space and figure. The hieratic pose, the remote dreamlike stare, and the faint suggestion of a crown-like tiara on the head of de Kooning's voluptuous seated woman suggest the presence of a symbol, like a playing card queen or a model in a magazine, rather than a specific person.

JACKSON POLLOCK (American, 1912–1956)

Male and Female, 1942–43
Oil on canvas, 73¼ x 48¹⁵⁄₁₆ inches
Gift of Mr. and Mrs. H. Gates Lloyd

Male and Female made its public appearance in
November 1943 in Pollock's stunning first exhibition
at Art of This Century, the innovative gallery run by
art patron Peggy Guggenheim. In a contemporary
statement about another painting, Pollock challenged
potential analysts of these enigmatic new pictures by
declaring that "any attempt on my part to say something about it . . . could only destroy it."[†] This statement offers a good deal of information: that Pollock
wished viewers to place faith in his paintings as mysterious, mystical beings, somewhat like silent gods
who reign over human beings yet are still vulnerable
to their words and deeds. His allusion to possible
destruction implies that, like a fire at risk of extin-
guishment, the painting is a vital force.

This yearning to believe in the power of art had drawn
the attention of Pollock and his young New York contemporaries to societies in which art had a magic
power. Their ethnographic curiosity was, in part,
inspired by the many European Surrealists in wartime
exile in New York, whose own experiments in "automatic," or improvisational, painting also intrigued the
Americans. Critics have attached significance to
Pollock's presence at a demonstration by Navajo sand
painters at the Museum of Modern Art the previous
year, but this was only part of his larger interest in art
that had a social function beyond that of decoration.
Pollock's title for this painting points to the fundamental forces he wanted it to conjure. The male is probably embodied in the black columnar form at right,
with its mysterious arithmetic graffiti; the female in the
curvy form at left, with marvelous eyelashes and round
breasts displaced as Picasso might have done. Both
figures, standing on tiny triangular feet, form a single
blocky construction in a whorl of splashes, smears,
and stripes that develops the energy immanent in the
two vertical figures. Pollock has sparked a painting by
rubbing together two opposing elemental forces, eter-
nally interdependent and often explosive.

81

JOSEPH CORNELL (American, 1903–1972)

Homage to Juan Gris, c. 1953–54
Box construction: wood, cut paper, and found objects,
18½ x 12½ x 4⅝ inches
Purchased for the John D. McIlhenny Collection

Cornell was a virtuoso of the quintessentially modern genres of collage and assemblage. This box is an early example in a large series of works Cornell made during the 1950s and 1960s devoted to the Spanish painter Juan Gris. Gris is one of the few modern artists who provided the subject for Cornell's collections, musings, and constructions; his better-known obsessions center on nineteenth-century divas and ballerinas or contemporary movie stars. We do not know the exact nature of Cornell's admiration for Gris, although his notes tell us that his original inspiration was a painting by Gris he saw at the Sidney Janis Gallery in New York. But the affinity is understandable: far more than that of other Cubists, Gris's sensibility was poetic and intimate, and the objects in his paintings and collages were invested with personal sentiment. Gris's death at the age of forty tinged his life with the romantic aura that deeply intrigued Cornell.

Dating from the early 1950s, this box features clear imagery in a sparse interior. The white paper cockatoo glued to a wooden backing is the common element shared by most of these boxes, and the pages from a French encyclopedia of history (on the back of the box) and literature (on its interior) testify to both artists' shared passion for French culture. The most explicitly Cubist component of the box is the miniature collage composition behind the bird, complete with motifs found in Gris's own great collages of the teens, such as the newspaper masthead, the wood graining, and the beautiful bit of blue sky and white cloud. Cornell's tribute to Gris conjures an air of quiet dignity and gentle mystery, as he honors an artistic legacy he could both appreciate and extend in his chosen medium.

DOROTHEA TANNING (American, born 1910)

Birthday, 1942
Oil on canvas, 40¼ x 25½ inches
Purchased with funds contributed by
Charles K. Williams III

Birthday is an announcement, a self-portrait hailing the arrival of an artist who emerged into the public eye with a fully formulated vision and an exquisitely flawless technique. Tanning, thirty-two years old, was working as a freelance illustrator for Manhattan department stores while pursuing her own painting in her Greenwich Village apartment. Tanning's artistic resolve had been catalyzed by the exhibition "Fantastic Art, Dada and Surrealism" at the Museum of Modern Art in 1936 and the attendant visibility of such work in New York's avant-garde circles. According to Tanning, *Birthday* was titled by the Surrealist émigré artist Max Ernst, who encountered it on her easel while scouting for works for gallery owner Peggy Guggenheim's upcoming exhibition of art made by women. Captivated by the model as well as by the painting, Ernst would become her husband and lifelong admirer of her work.

Although the painting presents an astonishing likeness of the artist, this portrayal does far more to create a character than to reveal a preexisting one. An exotically dressed, unsmiling young woman stands on a deeply tilted floor grasping a white porcelain doorknob. Although she is solidly, precisely set in space, that space is more dream than reality, with its shimmering mother-of-pearl light, its infinite recession of doors, and its extraordinary perspective. The woman's ruffled purple brocade jacket, opened to reveal her bare chest, tops a skirt of long green tendrils, which, upon scrutiny, assume the form of human bodies. She is attended by an ally, a fantastic furry creature with wings and a long tail, ready to accompany her on the adventures that lie beyond the doors.

BEAUFORD DELANEY (American, 1901–1979)

Portrait of James Baldwin, 1945
Oil on canvas, 22 x 18 inches
Purchased with funds contributed by the Dietrich
Foundation in memory of Joseph C. Bailey, and with
a grant from The Judith Rothschild Foundation

James Baldwin and Beauford Delaney first met in down-
town New York in 1941. Delaney was a forty-year-old
artist whose cityscapes and portraits had recently
achieved their first mainstream acclaim. Baldwin was
only sixteen years old, a troubled high-school senior
who had been advised by a friend to seek out Delaney
as a source of advice. The two developed an instant
rapport and Delaney introduced the future writer to the
worlds of music and poetry as well as art. When they
both eventually joined the growing circle of African
American expatriates in Paris, the role of guiding spirit
reversed. Baldwin served as a notable advocate of
Delaney's painting and an invaluable friend during the
last twenty-five years of the older man's life, a period
when he was plagued by mental and physical illness.
Delaney viewed Baldwin as a spiritual son, and Baldwin
later would call Delaney his "principal witness." The
term could be understood literally: over the course of
the next thirty years, Delaney portrayed Baldwin in at
least ten drawings and paintings.

Baldwin's many eloquent descriptions of Delaney's
work call attention to the uncanny power of light in
his paintings. In this commanding portrayal of 1945,
the face of the twenty-one-year-old man shines forth
from the canvas like a beacon. Its intensity recalls
the portraits of Van Gogh, whom Delaney revered.
The piercing eyes, the strongly defined nose and lips,
and the trunk-like neck give Baldwin the unforgettable
presence of an icon, as does the close-up viewpoint of
the composition. The daringly juxtaposed passages
of raw color create a palpable electricity emanating
from the mind and heart of this young man who would
create such major literary achievements as *Go Tell It
on the Mountain* (1952), *Giovanni's Room* (1956), and
Another Country (1962).

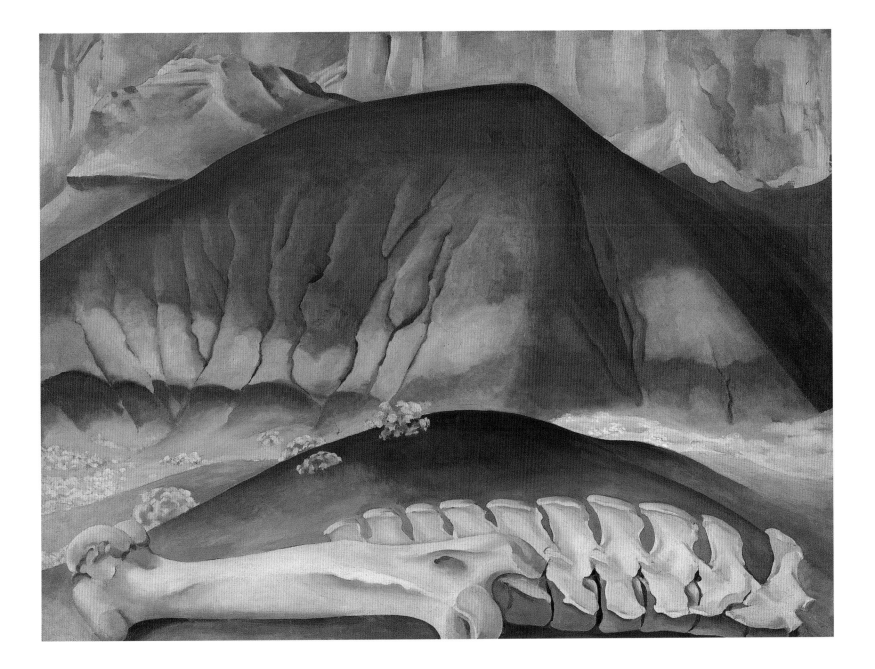

GEORGIA O'KEEFFE (American, 1887–1986)

Red Hills and Bones, 1941
Oil on canvas, 29¾ x 40 inches
The Alfred Stieglitz Collection

Red Hills and Bones is one of the many interpretations of the New Mexico landscape that Georgia O'Keeffe painted over the course of six decades. Living in Manhattan, she began in 1929 to spend summers in the American Southwest. The American modernist artists championed by her husband, Alfred Stieglitz, were very much preoccupied with the need to invent a distinctly native modern aesthetic. Many of them found their primary sources in the urban cityscape of New York City, but O'Keeffe turned to the far-off landscape for indigenous inspiration.

Here she sets an arrangement of bleached bones— a cow's leg bone and spinal column—against the dry, cracked red earth of the hills that surrounded her New Mexico home. Across the horizontal composition stretch three echoing forms: the large red hill, the small brown mound in the mid-ground, and the arc of white bones immediately before the viewer. This trio implies a progression of aging; the large red hill, split with erosion to suggest folds of wrinkled skin, seems to have decomposed to reveal a spine that stretched beneath and supported the once-fertile landscape. The small bunches of flowers scattered over the small brown mound suggest the renewal of life from decay.

O'Keeffe's highly focused rendering of her landscape, to the complete exclusion of the wide Southwestern sky, recalls the close-up views of flower blossoms from the 1920s for which she is most often celebrated. This intensely cropped composition monumentalizes the simplicity of organic forms and ultimately confirms their symbolic power. O'Keeffe's rich palette of reds, oranges, browns, and yellows evokes the earth itself, as if she dipped her paintbrush into the soil as she stood before her subject.

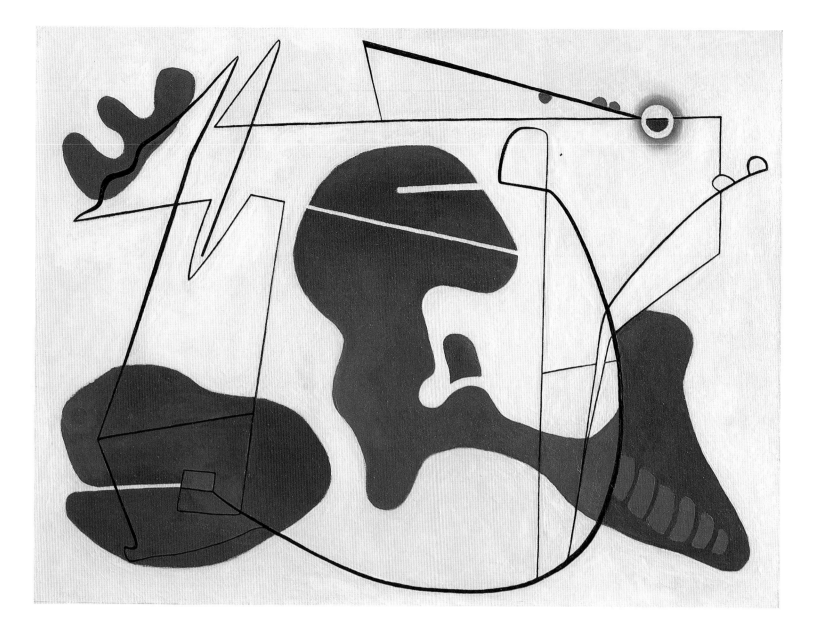

ALICE TRUMBULL MASON (American, 1904–1971)

Brown Shapes White, 1941
Oil on panel, 24 x 31¾ inches
A. E. Gallatin Collection

Alice Trumbull Mason was a founding member of
the American Abstract Artists, a cooperative group
of painters and sculptors who started exhibiting
together in 1937. Sharing a common desire to
promote abstract art in the United States during the
turmoil of the Depression years, these artists drew
their inspiration from recent developments in abstract
art in Europe at a time when the regionalism of American scene painters was promoted almost exclusively

by gallery owners and critics. Mason had developed
an abstract painting style as early as 1929 while
studying under Arshile Gorky at the Grand Central
School of Art in New York.

The reductive simplicity, ambiguous spatial relationships, and subtle color of *Brown Shapes White* define
it as a classic example of Mason's "architectural" abstraction, which she described as "making colour, density, dark and light, rhythm and balance work together
without depending on references and associations."[†]
The painting is composed of floating brown shapes,
the largest of which is delicately shaded with ocher
gills, interconnected by whiplash black lines. This imagery is dispersed across the entire field of the canvas

and set against a white ground that functions as both
depth and surface. The liveliness of the painting's design comes from the complex interplay between the
irregular organic forms and the linear geometric scaffolding. In 1942 A. E. Gallatin, himself a dedicated
abstract painter, gave Mason her first solo exhibition
at his Museum of Living Art, installed in a study room
at New York University, and later donated this work to
the Philadelphia Museum of Art as part of his collection of international modernism.

STUART DAVIS (American, 1892–1964)

Something on the Eight Ball, 1953–54
Oil on canvas, 56 x 45 inches
Purchased with the Adele Haas Turner and Beatrice
Pastorius Turner Memorial Fund

The intense colors and floating abstract shapes of this
jubilant picture seem to jump off the canvas with the
visual punch of an advertising poster. In the 1950s
Davis began to resuscitate earlier motifs, often over-
laying his boisterous, cosmopolitan imagery on top of
the basic framework of his Cubist paintings from the
1920s. Exemplifying Davis's dialogue with the art of
his own past, *Something on the Eight Ball* revisits an
earlier painting entitled *Matches,* a still life that focused
on three books of matches clustered in the center of
the canvas. The artist reintroduced these matchbook
forms in the later painting, placing them on a dynamic
yellow ground and adding a horizontal matchstick in
the middle of the picture. The original composition was
then transformed by the generous distribution of
bright, silhouetted, colorful shapes—like the collages
of cut-out paper and gouache Matisse was making at
the same time—that take the form of a teeming
jumble of lines, squiggles, numbers, and words.
Davis's cursive letters are in themselves color forms,
and the incorporation of the words "any," "IT," and
"facilities" gives the picture the feel of the accelerated
pace of urban life.

Davis explained the title in a letter to Henry Clifford,
former curator of paintings at the Philadelphia Museum
of Art: "*Something on the Eight Ball* is a switch on the
usual phrase 'behind the eight ball.' I used it without
knowledge of hearing it before in a conversation with
some jazz musicians [and] it got a laugh, causing me
to remember it."[†] The references to pool and jazz
reflect the artist's enthusiasm for American vernacular
culture, an integral presence in paintings that were
"Pop" ahead of their time.

MILTON AVERY (American, 1893–1965)

Black Jumper, 1944
Oil on canvas, 54³/₁₆ x 33³/₄ inches
Bequest of Mrs. Maurice J. Speiser in memory of
Raymond A. Speiser

The model for this painting was the artist's twelve-year-
old daughter, March. Avery first painted his daughter
when she was one week old and made so many pictures of her while she was growing up that in 1947
the Durand-Ruel Galleries in New York staged an exhibition of his work called simply, "My Daughter, March."
Black Jumper is a classic example of the artist's ma-
ture style, in which figures and objects are divested
of identifying detail and flattened and distorted to
become interlocking shapes in a strictly articulated
design, like a child's jigsaw puzzle. Avery situated his
daughter within a domestic interior made up of luminous masses of saturated color, which combine to
create an extremely shallow pictorial space. Each element has been reduced to a broad, flat expanse comprised of a single, vibrant color: for example, the red
table, the cobalt-green wall, the purple blouse, and
the yellow screen that contains the artist's signature.
These pairs of complementary colors maximize the
visual impact of the painting. Its rich palette and formal simplicity can be compared to earlier paintings by
Henri Matisse, especially the French artist's portraits
of the late 1930s, which convey a similar interest
in abstract patterning.

Avery's work communicates, in his own words, "the
ecstasy of the moment," which he hoped to achieve
by seizing one sharp instant in nature, in this case
the awkwardness of a gangly adolescent trying on
her new clothes, and capturing it by means of simplified forms and radiant color harmonies. With her legs
planted defiantly apart and her hands clasped demurely
in front of her, March's form dominates the composition. Although Avery left her face blank, generalizing
the figure to a universal type or essence, *Black Jumper*
remains a tender portrayal of a proud father's love
for his daughter.

ALICE NEEL (American, 1900–1984)

Last Sickness, 1953
Oil on canvas, 30 x 22 inches
Promised gift of Richard Neel and Hartley S. Neel

Last Sickness is one of only four portraits that Neel
painted of her mother, Alice Hartley Neel. Mrs. Neel
lived most of her life in Colwyn, Pennsylvania, just outside Philadelphia, where Alice was born and raised.
This painting was made while she was staying at her
daughter's home in New York during her final months.
With heartrending directness, the portrait conveys the
loneliness and fear of an elderly person facing death.
Despite the occasion of a portrait sitting, vanity is
nowhere in evidence; the model is too worn out to
try to look cheerful or proud. But Neel deftly captured
the intelligent sparkle that remained in her mother's
eyes and her skeptical curiosity in the face of this
peculiar encounter between mother and daughter.

The honesty and compassion evident in Neel's portrayal of her mother reflect the roots of her art in the
tradition of social realism, and particularly its flowering
in Greenwich Village during the 1930s. Those artistic
convictions never left her, even as the mainstream art
world entered an era dominated by the forms and
rhetoric of abstract painting. Neel's interest remained
focused on the portrayal of the human condition, but
she cultivated a virtuosity that delighted in lavishing
painterly attention on the pink and red plaid of her
mother's flannel bathrobe.

Her family provided a central subject for Neel, whose
apartments doubled as studios throughout her life,
and for whom painting was as much a part of an ordinary day as sharing conversations and meals. Painting
family portraits began with those of her children, continued with their wives and children, and at the end of
her life when she had achieved renown, encompassed
a new extended family of art critics, art historians,
collectors, and fellow artists.

BEN SHAHN (American, born Lithuania, 1898–1969)

Miners' Wives, c. 1948
Tempera on panel, 48 x 36 inches
Gift of Wright S. Ludington

Miners' Wives is one of four paintings and nearly one hundred drawings created by Shahn in response to a mining disaster in Centralia, Illinois, in 1947. Like much of the artist's enduring imagery of this period, this painting originated in a commercial assignment. Shahn's illustrations for an article on the explosion at the Centralia Number 5 mine appeared in the March 1948 issue of *Harper's Magazine,* in which the journalist John Bartlow Martin exposed the gross negligence and bureaucratic ineptitude that resulted in the deaths of 111 miners in a coal-dust explosion. The artist then reworked and expanded his spare and compassionate drawings as the subject matter for tempera paintings, which also drew upon contemporary news media photographs of the tragedy.[†]

The powerful impact of Shahn's painting stems, in part, from his decision to focus on the aftermath of the catastrophe, in particular the devastation brought to the miners' families, rather than the blast itself. The artist conflated several episodes from Martin's account to depict the heart-wrenching scene of two women in the mine washhouse, mutely awaiting news of their husbands' fates. The ashen faced woman in the foreground, whose massive hands are clenched in grief-stricken agony, anguishes over their hopeless situation. Behind her, seated beneath the trousers her husband would have put on after his shift, a woman holds a child in her lap. In the background, two departing mine officials have the solemn appearance of undertakers.

ANDREW NEWELL WYETH (American, born 1917)

Groundhog Day, 1959
Tempera on Masonite, 31⅜ x 32⅛ inches
Gift of Henry F. du Pont and Mrs. John Wintersteen

Andrew Wyeth has turned repeatedly to the rural countryside and people of his native Chadds Ford, Pennsylvania, as subjects for his paintings. This picture takes
us into the light-flooded kitchen of the artist's neighbors,
Karl and Anna Kuerner, whom Wyeth had known since
childhood. Wyeth painted the work in egg tempera, a
painstaking medium that demands patience as well as
skill. The artist's meticulous craftsmanship enabled
him to render with exquisite clarity every detail of the
farmyard kitchen and the crisp winter landscape outside the window. "That February day," he remembered,
"the sun's rays caught the corner of the table that
was set for dinner, awaiting the return of Mr. Kuerner
from a farm sale in Lancaster. That is how it started."[†]
The painting exemplifies the artist's consummate ability to translate simple objects to a higher plane of
emotional feeling. The stark simplicity of the German
immigrant farmer's life is encapsulated in the white cup
and saucer, plate, and single knife (the only utensil he
used for eating) laid out on the pristine tablecloth
for his noonday meal.

The original composition for *Groundhog Day* included
the farmer's fierce German shepherd, but Wyeth later
painted out the dog. The animal's bared fangs were
transformed into the splintered end of the roughly
hewn log seen through the window and placed along-
side heavy chains and a barbed wire fence, which
combine to create a menacing atmosphere at odds
with the quiet solitude of the still-life arrangement on
the table. The subtle nuances of tone and light, painted
with a muted palette of pale yellows, pure whites,
and earthy browns and tans, sharpen the eye to the
cold isolation and raw beauty of the place. The harsh
sunlight filtering through the window portends a long
winter since, as the title suggests, the proverbial
groundhog would surely see his shadow on such a
bright February second morning.

DAVID ALFARO SIQUEIROS (Mexican, 1896–1974)

War, 1939
Duco and enamel on two panels,
each 48 x 31⅝ inches
Gift of Ines Amor

Siqueiros's life was equally devoted to painting and radical politics. The artist took up arms in 1936 to fight for the republican army in the Spanish Civil War, the conflict that spurred him to paint *War* when he returned to Mexico in 1939. Through his involvement in the mural movement in Mexico, Los Angeles, and New York, he not only gave public expression to his political ideals but also was led to experiment with new materials and formats that profoundly influenced all of his work, including panel paintings such as *War.* It is one of eleven works realized in duco paint, or synthetic lacquer, exhibited in Siqueiros's first solo exhibition in New York at the Pierre Matisse Gallery in 1940.

War combines the compressed distortions and ambiguities of Cubist space with a depiction of a monumental, heroic nude body. Using anatomy and musculature as well as shadow and light, the artist has crafted an image of anguish with the female body representing a nation in ruins, inflamed by conflict, and shattered by suffering. The figure, stretched across two compact panels, is shown lying on a red carpet with rivulets and ridges evoking a river of blood. Her calves, toes, shoulders, and right hand are taut and contorted with pain that flows from her flayed left forearm and hand. Represented in deadly gray, the arm is open to the bone, where the picture surface reveals heavily built-up paint layers and raw board. The texture, created from layers of gesso as well as duco paint and enamel spray paint, reinforces the materiality of the massive body. Molten red and creamy white colors suffuse the painting with sizzling energy. The artist's highly sculptural rendering of the subject imbues this portable picture with a mural-like power.

JACQUES LIPCHITZ (American, born Lithuania, 1891–1973)

Prometheus Strangling the Vulture, 1944
Bronze, stone base, height with base 96½ inches
Purchased with the Lisa Norris Elkins Fund

This dynamic sculpture dramatizes Lipchitz's personal revision of the Greek myth of Prometheus, who stole fire from the gods and brought it to man. In his fury at the theft, Zeus sent an eagle to pluck out the liver of the audacious rebel. According to the myth, Prometheus is rescued by Hercules. In Lipchitz's version, Prometheus himself vanquishes the bird (transposed to a vulture), grasping its talons and throat with his two hands.

Prometheus functions as an autobiographical telling of Lipchitz's own artistic struggles. The story dates back to a sculpture he made as a commission for the Paris World's Fair of 1937. Having abandoned his earlier Cubist style, Lipchitz created a work of robust volumes he found appropriate to a monumental work of mythological force. During a grim time, the sculpture seemed to him a necessary reminder of heroism in the face of assault. Unfortunately, soon after its display at the fair, the sculpture was mutilated by an attacker and destroyed. Lipchitz's subsequent version, made for a government building in Rio de Janeiro in 1944, was also ill fated: without the artist's involvement, the model was poorly cast into a bronze that Lipchitz promptly repudiated.

In 1952 Lipchitz entered the plaster model for his Brazil commission in the annual sculpture exhibition at the Pennsylvania Academy of the Fine Arts, Philadelphia, where it won the grand prize. The day after he sent the piece to Philadelphia, his New York studio was ruined by fire. Inspired by their respect for the sculpture and by its narrow escape, the trustees of the Philadelphia Museum of Art commissioned Lipchitz to cast the plaster in bronze. Its presence on the front steps of the Museum salutes a sculptor who personally overcame obstacles. The triumph of the fire-bearer Prometheus, often regarded in mythology as the first artist, speaks for all those whose work is displayed in the building beyond.

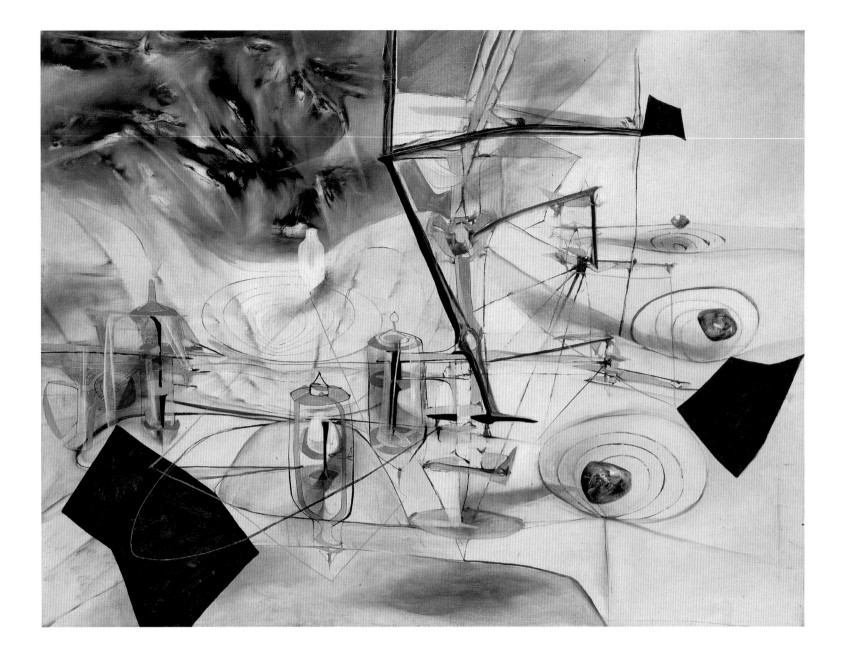

ROBERTO MATTA (Chilean, born 1911)

The Bachelors Twenty Years After, 1943
Oil on canvas, 38 x 40 inches
Purchased with the Edith H. Bell Fund and the Edward
and Althea Budd Fund; gifts (by exchange) of Mr. and
Mrs. William P. Wood and Bernard Davis; and bequest
(by exchange) of Anna Warren Ingersoll

This painting pays homage to Marcel Duchamp's great
allegory of frustrated desire, *The Bride Stripped Bare
by Her Bachelors, Even (The Large Glass)*. Matta
admired the French artist's explorations of science
and eroticism, and his painting continues the themes
that Duchamp had abandoned in 1923, when he
declared his *Large Glass* to be "definitively unfinished."

Twenty years later, the bachelors are energized by the
Chilean artist's infinite space and incisive linear markings, recalling the symmetrical cracks in the original
work, which occurred when the two sheets of glass
were accidentally smashed. The sexual tension that
permeates the *Large Glass* is translated into an explosive electromagnetic force field, as the excitement of
the transparent, lamplike bachelors generates an illuminating gas that mixes with other nebulous vapors
to produce a vision of primary chaos, with slivers of
stormy crystalline light. Matta created this evocative
imagery by spilling thin washes of lemon yellow and
green paint on the canvas, wiping the surface with a
rag, and then drawing with a paintbrush to define
the mechanical–organic elements.

This painting is one of a series that Matta called "Psychological Morphologies," in which the artist sought to
discover regions of space hitherto unexplored in the
realm of art. Morphology, a science dealing with the
metamorphoses of forms, established the atmosphere
of continuous transformation that characterized Matta's
early work in Paris, where he was a prominent figure
in the Surrealist movement. *The Bachelors Twenty
Years After* was painted in the United States, where
Matta had moved in 1939 following the outbreak of
World War II in Europe. The presence in New York of
this *enfant terrible* of Surrealism had a catalytic effect
on the younger generation of American avant-garde
artists, in particular the future Abstract Expressionist
painters Robert Motherwell and Arshile Gorky.

ARSHILE GORKY (American, born Armenia, 1904–1948)

Dark Green Painting, c. 1948
Oil on canvas, 43¾ x 55½ inches
Gift (by exchange) of Mr. and Mrs. Rodolphe Meyer de Schauensee and Mr. and Mrs. R. Sturgis Ingersoll

Arshile Gorky, born Vasdanig Adoian in Armenia, was one in the array of immigrants to the city who created the so-called New York School. He came to New England as a teenager and moved to New York in 1925 at the age of twenty-one. Gorky then spent fifteen years devotedly absorbing the work of the great European masters, painting "with," as he said,

Cézanne, Picasso, and others. He broke through to a unique voice only in the 1940s and in a short span of time (ended by his suicide in 1948) produced an intense, brilliant body of work. Steeped in memories of his homeland, his paintings employ an utterly contemporary vocabulary of abstract forms that possess the force of symbols but resist literal decoding.

Dark Green Painting is one of Gorky's very last works. In retrospect, its dense surface and somber palette hint at tragedy. The artist's sophisticated use of unexpected colors is as remarkable here as in his luminous works of the early 1940s. Gorky is one of the great draftsmen of the twentieth century, and that quality is revealed as much in paintings such as this one as in

his large body of drawings. His fluid field of fragmented and hovering shapes suggests what might be interpreted as an "automatic" composition. But, as in the case of much modern work once believed to have been freely improvised—ranging from the floating fields of Joan Miró to the allover surfaces of Jackson Pollock—this composition was intensely planned down to each detail. A large-scale drawing in pencil and crayon meticulously plots on a gridded page the design of the painting to follow. While the painter wished his work to look as though it sprang directly from his unconscious, the ability to convey that impression required a level of control and virtuosity developed over years of intense discipline.

WILLIAM BAZIOTES (American, 1912–1963)

Night, 1953
Oil on canvas, 19¾ x 24³⁄₁₆ inches
Gift of Anne d'Harnoncourt Rishel

Using delicate washes of color and imagery culled from nature, from paleontology, and from his own free associations, Baziotes invented a new type of landscape painting in the 1940s. He was one of the first of his generation to make contact with the émigré Surrealist painters in New York, where he moved from Reading, Pennsylvania, in 1933. Baziotes balanced the Surrealists' advocacy of spontaneity with imagery

he retained from his visits to the American Museum of Natural History in New York, a laboratory that fueled the imaginations of many artists at the time. In sparse, horizonless compositions of simple biomorphic shapes, he evoked a liquid underworld of plants and organisms and the atmosphere of primeval life as natural metaphors for inner psychic realms.

Baziotes remained absorbed by the Surrealist search for poetic and painterly correspondences for the unconscious into the 1950s, when he withdrew into isolation from his peers. During this decade he completed only a small number of paintings each year, and the works themselves suggest a more thoughtful,

meditative working process in which he distilled the elements of his pictures to a few essential components. Painted during this culminating period, *Night* derives its power from subtly gauged, diaphanous color harmonies and the quiet drama that results from the placement of its few simple shapes and its wiry linear web. Haunting and amorphous, the imagery of *Night* transports the viewer to a dreamy state of contemplation, leaving much open to imaginative interpretation.

LEE KRASNER (American, 1908–1984)

Composition, 1949
Oil on canvas, 38 1/16 x 27 13/16 inches
Gift of the Aaron E. Norman Fund, Inc.

As an ambitious artist in New York City during the heyday of Abstract Expressionism, Krasner was committed to a serious career, which sometimes competed
with her role as a supportive wife to America's most
famous postwar painter, Jackson Pollock. Shortly after
their marriage in 1945 the couple moved to
Easthampton, New York, distancing themselves from
the maelstrom of the New York art world. In the country both artists began painting with renewed vigor.
Pollock worked in a separate barn that served as his
studio, and Krasner, in their home. *Composition* is one
of the paintings in the breakthrough series she created
in the late 1940s called "Little Image" paintings.

Meticulously crafted and intimately scaled, *Composition* reflects Krasner's deft control of new, unorthodox
painting methods. Working with her canvas flat on a
table, painting with sticks or a palette knife and dripping paint from a can or using it straight from the tube,
Krasner arrived at a surprisingly controlled-looking
picture that incorporates both drawing and writing.
Its densely textured surface is covered with delicate
webs of overlapping skeins of dripped white paint
forming small compartments of squares, triangles,
and circles, some filled in with elaborate designs.
These miniature signs are layered on top of a thickly
built-up slab of yellow, green, red, and brown pigments
to make a gritty tabletlike construction suggesting the
visual symbols of archaic societies. Impenetrable and
unreadable, this work celebrates painting as a primal
means of communication through an analogy to
picture-based writing codes that presage the
development of alphabets.

ADOLPH GOTTLIEB (American, 1903–1974)

The Cadmium Sound, 1954
Oil on canvas, 60¹⁄₁₆ x 72¼ inches
Purchased with the Edward and Althea Budd Fund

The Cadmium Sound is one of a small group of exuberant, gestural paintings created by Gottlieb in 1954 and 1955. Its graffiti-like immediacy reflects the artist's experimentation with "automatic writing" or "psychic automatism," a technique explored by European Surrealists and based on the idea that painting and drawing freely or even distractedly could express thoughts buried in the subconscious. Extending this idea in new formal directions, Gottlieb created a group of pictures characterized by their latticed structure and dominant black color. Nicknamed "labyrinths" because of their ambiguous pathways, works such as this incorporate recognizable signs and symbols into Gottlieb's unique abstract calligraphy.

The artist layered at least two different applications of black paint—one watery thin, the other more dense and reflective—on the yellow wash ground, accenting the topmost linear web with bright white lead pigment. The unexpected spatial effects he obtained result from his controlled exploitation of unpredictable aspects of the painting process. Gottlieb incorporated different basic signs into his allover composition, including stars, arrows, and even faces, but the graphic energy and immediacy of the picture are more significant than direct translation of these discrete symbols. The title, _The Cadmium Sound,_ evokes both the vibrant yellow cadmium pigment that Gottlieb applied to the uppermost stratum of his composition and its seemingly immeasurable atmospheric depth.

ROBERT MOTHERWELL (American, 1915–1991)

Elegy to the Spanish Republic, 1958–60
Oil and charcoal on canvas, 78 x 99½ inches
Gift (by exchange) of Miss Anna Warren Ingersoll and
partial gift of the Dedalus Foundation, Inc.

In his career-long series of paintings and works
on paper entitled "Elegy to the Spanish Republic,"
Motherwell used the tragic consequences of the
Spanish Civil War as a vehicle for exploring archetypal
themes of freedom and loss. Motherwell was only
twenty-one years old when the war broke out in 1936,
but the traumatic conflict between the democratically
elected republican government and Franco's Fascist

armed forces made an indelible impression on him.
Motherwell began the "Spanish Elegy" series in 1948,
when he illustrated a poem for a never-published issue
of the magazine *Possibilities*. The starkness of the
imagery and the symbolic use of color—the smolder-
ing blackness of death and the vital whiteness of life—
presented the artist with a somber yet powerful visual
statement capable of infinite variations that would be
explored in his work over the next four decades.

Motherwell was very attached to this version and always
kept it in his studio as a catalyst for new pictures. The
pared-down composition, consisting of a massive column of funereal black that separates the three oval
shapes, is a masterpiece of tension and balance. The

work's raw, aggressive atmosphere is intensified by
the splatters and drips of paint and the irregular, freely
brushed edges of the forms. Motherwell's monumental
painting communicates his passionate feelings about
the doomed Spanish republican cause. However, like
Goya and Manet before him, Motherwell went beyond
the specific tragedy of war to create a haunting
meditation on life and death.

MARK DI SUVERO (American, born 1933)

Amerigo for My Father, 1963
Wood, steel, iron, and clothesline,
102 x 78 x 60 inches
Gift of Mr. and Mrs. David N. Pincus

Mark di Suvero's signature works of the 1960s were created from discarded beams and planks collected at demolition sites near his Fulton Street studio in Manhattan. These sculptures balance the monumental and the precarious in dramatic compositions of criss-crossing elements projecting into space. The architectural components that the artist scavenged and transformed into sculpture push the spontaneity, grandeur, and raw energy of Abstract Expressionism into three-dimensional space, marrying the spatial dynamics of gestural painting to a new aesthetic of found objects drawn from the detritus of urban life.

Di Suvero brought the principles of his gigantic outdoor sculptural projects into the making of *Amerigo for My Father,* a work scaled for presentation in a gallery. Composed of two cast-off timbers with rusted metal bolts and clamps, an I beam welded to the central supporting pipe, and a beam emerging from a metal plate on the floor, the piece is cacophonous and aggressive yet self-contained. Two cantilevered metal pieces, mangled and attached to a horizontal beam, jut into space. An ordinary clothesline is suspended from one. An upside-down chair hangs at the end of the clothesline, one of a number of suspended moveable objects that the artist incorporated in sculptures during the early 1960s. Amid the hefty, gravity-bound solidity of the sculpture, this element of domestic furniture is like a child's swing discovered in the midst of a construction site, and it imparts a sense of poignancy and playfulness to di Suvero's masculine junkyard aesthetic. This counterpoint of homespun familiarity continues in the title, *Amerigo for My Father,* in which the artist pays tribute to his heritage as the son of Venetian parents.

FRANZ KLINE (American, 1910–1962)

Torches Mauve, 1960
Oil on canvas, 120⅛ x 81⅛ inches
Gift of the artist

The enormous scaffolded structures of Franz Kline's paintings epitomize many aspects of Abstract Expressionism: mural scale, innovative brushwork, allover imagery, and dense space. The artist's powerful, sweeping strokes were often created with a four-inch-wide housepainting brush, which in his early days he would load with whatever paint he could get his hands on. In the late 1950s at the urging of his dealer, Sidney Janis, Kline began to use high-quality tube paint, purchased from Joseph Torch's art supply store at 147 West 14th Street in New York. Torch sold his own brand of "permanent artists' oil colors," made to his specifications, and this work adopts its title (though slightly transformed) from the mauve oil paint that Kline used to paint it.

The artist's earlier abstractions took form primarily in stark configurations of black and white. Kline had shied away from exhibiting paintings incorporating his favorite blues, lemon yellows, and deep mauves until he found a way to give color the monumental presence and raw emotional power of black and white. *Torches Mauve* is an early example of that breakthrough. Kline's bravura handling of paint is evident in the variegated surface texture, which appears to have been painted very quickly. In several passages Kline applied the paint thickly, as he built the architectonic structure of the work out of great slabs of black, like girders, only to scrape through the wet surface with a palette knife to admit light and air into otherwise opaque spaces. The atmospheric flashes of mauve deepen the mood of Kline's painting, imparting a sense of towering strength and epic grandeur.

HANS HOFMANN (American, born Germany, 1880–1966)

Lumen Naturale, 1962
Oil on canvas, 84 x 78 inches
Purchased with the John Howard McFadden, Jr., Fund

Lumen Naturale comes from Hans Hofmann's last body of work. In 1956 he adopted a structure of overlapping, floating rectangles as the basis for his work. One hallmark of his postwar style—extravagant, all-over mark-making—now took a secondary role in relationship to his use of these straight-edged shapes and bright colors. He spent many summers painting on Cape Cod and remained inspired by nature and landscape even as he devoted himself to a reduced vocabulary of form and space, light and color. This ongoing search for painterly equivalents to natural effects is suggested by the title Hofmann invented for this rigorous yet lively picture: "natural light." As photographs show, Hofmann worked out his formal compositions by experimenting with paper cut-outs of shapes pinned temporarily to the canvas. By juxtaposing vibrant hues realized with different densities of pigment, often applied with a palette knife, he transposed elements of the collage method to the medium of colored paint.

In Europe and America, Hofmann was renowned as a teacher as well as an artist. He emigrated from Munich to New York in 1931, opening a school in Greenwich Village in 1938 just around the corner from A. E. Gallatin's Museum of Living Art. The emphasis on creating dynamic pictorial space through abstract means, often nicknamed "push and pull," was central to Hofmann's contribution as teacher. *Lumen Naturale* is an excellent example of Hofmann's theory in action. The work was painted after he had stopped teaching to concentrate solely on his art work, and its tense spatial and coloristic relationships reveal Hofmann's investigations distilled to essentials.

MORRIS LOUIS (American, 1912–1962)

Beth, 1959–60
Acrylic resin on canvas, 105 x 106¼ inches
Purchased with the Adele Haas Turner and Beatrice
Pastorius Turner Memorial Fund

Morris Louis belongs to a second generation of
Abstract Expressionist artists who came to be known
as the color-field painters. They inherited the
expansive scale and nonrepresentational imagery of
painters like Jackson Pollock and Franz Kline. But
these artists rejected the vigorous brushwork and rich
textures favored by their predecessors, aiming instead
for an open color expression, free from tactile
associations. This imposing painting belongs to a
series of stained pictures known as the "Veils" that
Louis began making in 1954. The artist developed a
technique that allowed him to paint without using
brushes by staining unprimed canvas with Magna, a
new resin-based acrylic paint manufactured by his
friend Leonard Bocour. Louis allowed gravity to control
the flow of paint that he poured in vertical ribbons
down the raw canvas, which he manipulated by tilting
the fabric until the color soaked into the desired
configuration. The diluted acrylic paint dried quickly,
permitting the artist to superimpose wave upon wave
of translucent color washes without waiting long
intervals for drying.

The transparent layers of saturated color in this
painting reveal the extraordinary technical virtuosity
Louis had achieved by the end of the 1950s. The
successive waves of glowing reds and oranges,
overlaid with a dark unifying tone that gives the work
its mysterious shadowy depths, combine to produce a
hovering mass of pulsating colors suggestive of a wall
of flames or petals of a giant flower. This curtain of
intense, bleeding colors spreads out toward the edge
of the picture, where it is framed by an uneven border
of bare canvas. The painting was given the title *Beth*
by the artist's widow, who developed a numbering
system for Louis's "Veil" paintings derived from letters
in the Hebrew alphabet.

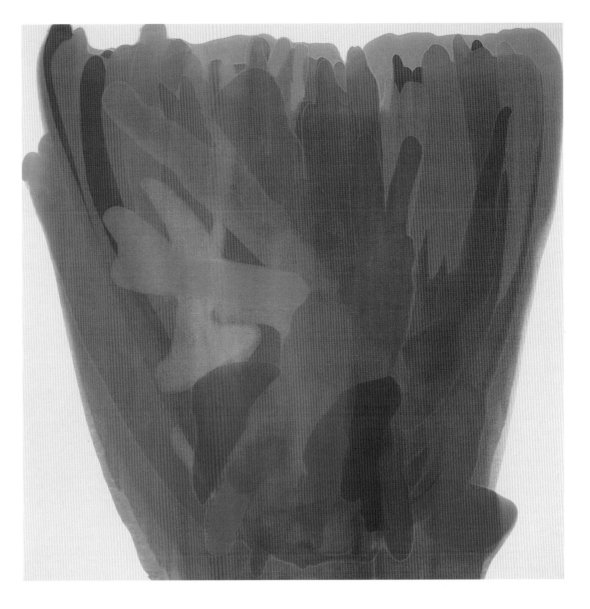

DAVID SMITH (American, 1906–1965)

2 Box Structure, 1961
Stainless steel, 165 x 53 x 27½ inches
Gift of Dr. and Mrs. Paul Todd Makler

In this towering work of spindly grace and ravishing surface effects, Smith explored the relationship between sculpture and painting. Originating in his experience creating spray-painted paper collages, the sculpture reflects the artist's procedure of welding together prefabricated steel parts to create spontaneous-looking compositions. Smith's interest in the dialogue between figuration and abstraction animates the sculpture with visual and psychological contrasts. From its nearly symmetrical balance of geometric shapes emerge two forceful personalities, on the left a figure with a lollipop-shaped head and on the right, a standing rectangle that suggests a painting on an easel, especially because of the calligraphic marks on its surface.

The delicate linear structure of *2 Box Structure* breaks out of the confines of its slim silhouette and demands that the viewer read the work both as a two-dimensional cutout and as a fully three-dimensional volume in space. The light effects that Smith achieved by burnishing its steel surface to an extremely high polish soften its angles and sharp edges and dissolve its solid massiveness into a flickering visual presence. Smith's innovative surface treatment continued in his last body of sculpture, the "Cubis" series, which *2 Box Structure* anticipates. As he explained shortly before his death: "This is the only time—in these stainless steel pieces—that I have ever been able to utilize light, and I depend a great deal on the reflective power of light. . . . It does have a semi-mirror reflection, and I like it (stainless steel) in that sense because no other material in sculpture can do that."[†]

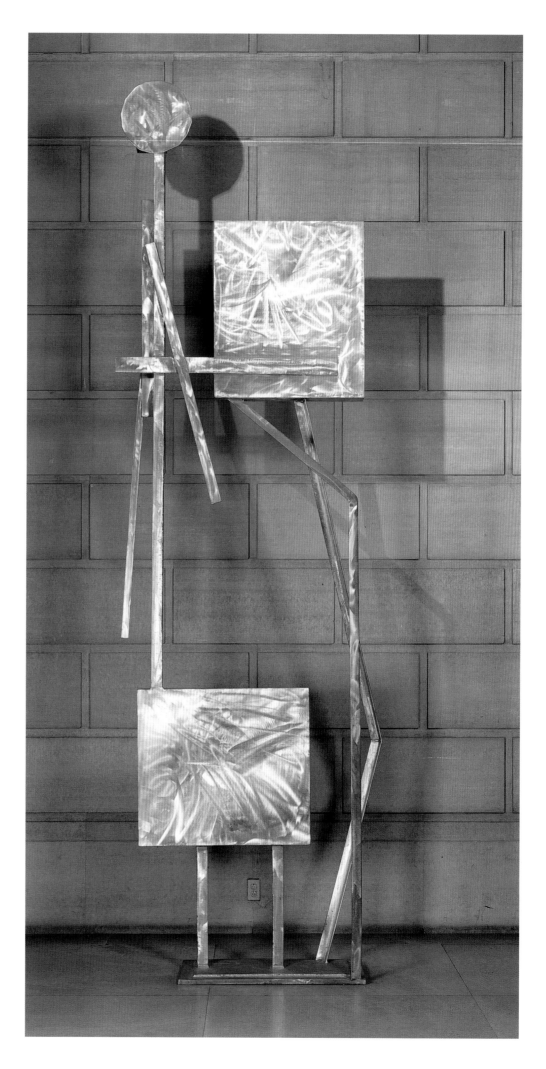

ALEXANDER CALDER (American, 1898–1976)

Ghost, 1964
Metal rods, painted sheet metal, length 34 feet
Purchased with the New Members Fund

Alexander Calder's mobiles brought the unique element of motion into the art of the twentieth century. Marcel Duchamp gave them their name on a visit to the American artist's Paris studio in 1931, specifically in reference to a small standing work that was electrically activated. Calder soon applied the term to any sculpture that moves, whether powered manually, by motor, or by air currents. The forms of Calder's

mobiles reflect his fascination with toys and his training as an engineer along with his early admiration for the imagery of Picasso, Mondrian, and Miró. The ubiquity of the mobile concept today, whether in the nursery or the corporate lobby, has obscured awareness of the radicalness of Calder's invention in the context of the history of sculpture.

Calder's early mobiles were domestically scaled, but by the 1950s they began to take on monumental proportions. The increase in size was a response to the demand for sculptures for public events or places, a result of the artist's great popularity as well as the building boom of postwar prosperity. Calder made

Ghost to hang high above the central rotunda of the Solomon R. Guggenheim Museum in New York, on the occasion of an exhibition of his work in 1964. The white color of the sheet-metal panels, which gives the enormous mobile its name, probably was inspired by the all-white interior of Frank Lloyd Wright's five-year-old Guggenheim building. *Ghost* now animates the Philadelphia Museum's Great Stair Hall, which offers a clear view of the Swann Memorial Fountain in Logan Circle (1924) made by his father, Alexander Stirling Calder, and the statue of William Penn atop City Hall (1894) made by his grandfather Alexander Milne Calder.

MARCEL DUCHAMP (American, born France, 1887–1968)

Given: 1. The Waterfall, 2. The Illuminating Gas (Étant donnés: 1. La chute d'eau, 2. Le gaz d'éclairage), 1946–66

Mixed media assemblage: old wooden door, bricks, velvet, wood, leather stretched over an armature of metal and other material, twigs, aluminum, iron, glass, Plexiglas, linoleum, cotton, electric lights, gas lamp, and motor, approximately 95½ x 70 x 49 inches
Gift of the Cassandra Foundation

Duchamp's final masterpiece, *Étant donnés,* has been described by the artist Jasper Johns as "the strangest work of art in any museum."[†] Permanently installed at the Philadelphia Museum of Art since 1969, this elaborate assemblage offers an unforgettable and untranslatable experience to those who peep through the two small holes in the old Spanish wooden door. The unsuspecting viewer encounters a spectacular sight: a naked woman lying spread-eagled on a bed of twigs and fallen leaves. In her left hand, this life-size mannequin holds aloft an old-fashioned gas lamp of the Bec Auer type, while behind her, in the far distance, a lush landscape rises toward the horizon. This illuminated backdrop consists of a retouched photograph of a hilly landscape with a dense cluster of trees outlined against a hazy turquoise sky. The only movement in the otherwise eerily still grotto is a sparkling waterfall, actually a flickering light source powered by an unseen motor, which pours into a lake on the right. The waterfall and the illuminating gas lamp are the elements "given" in the enigmatic title, which comes from one of Duchamp's earlier notes for *The Bride Stripped Bare by Her Bachelors, Even (The Large Glass),* suggesting an intimate connection between the themes of the two works.

The artist secretly constructed *Étant donnés* over a twenty-year period, during which it was generally assumed that Duchamp had given up making works of art. The piece was partly assembled from miscellaneous objects the artist collected with the assistance of his wife, Teeny. The couple visited demolition sites for bricks, the countryside around New York for twigs, and a small town near Cadaqués in Spain for the weather-worn door. These elements were transported to the artist's studio on 14th Street in New York, where their presence added to the trompe-l'oeil realism of the assemblage, which makes one think of voyeuristic peep shows or brightly lit dioramas in natural history museums. In accordance with Duchamp's wishes, the existence of *Étant donnés* became public only after his death, when the piece was installed at the Philadelphia Museum of Art following the artist's instructions.

107

JAMES ROSENQUIST (American, born 1933)

Zone, 1961
Oil on two canvas sections, each 95 x 47¹¹/₁₆ inches
Purchased with the Edith H. Bell Fund

Rosenquist has called this his first entirely Pop painting, created not long after he quit his job as a billboard artist working high above the streets of New York City. The odd juxtaposition of a woman's face with a dewy tomato exemplifies the artist's unique gift for meshing unlike forms. Rosenquist's training is evident in the flurry of broad brushstrokes he used to apply the gray, black, and white paint to the canvas, echoing the billboard technique of covering a vast surface area with layers of flat color. The oil paint is the type used by sign painters and may have been left over from the artist's day job, creating window-display backdrops at Tiffany & Co., Bloomingdale's, and other stores in New York.

The artist turned to what he called the world of supermarket junk and plenty for the imagery that makes up *Zone* and initiated his practice of using scraps of magazine advertisements selling such consumer items as fruit and cosmetics to make preparatory collages for his Pop art canvases. Pond's "all-new Angel Skin" beauty cream provided Rosenquist with the image of the alluring woman, whose hands "respond instantly and thrillingly" to the moisturizer. The clarity of the chic promotional ad is transformed in the finished painting by an enormous change in scale, which renders the painting's iconography virtually unrecognizable at first glance. The fragmented composition slowly reveals itself as a collision between the image of the Pond's model and the leafy tomato, shown in extreme close-up and sliced into distinct sections, or zones, by a zigzag line. Since the woman and tomato are dislocated from their expected contexts and portrayed with calculated coolness, it is difficult to tell if the woman is laughing or crying, or if the beads of moisture on the ripe fruit represent her tears or water droplets.

ROBERT RAUSCHENBERG (American, born 1925)

Estate, 1963
Oil and silk-screened inks on canvas,
96 x 69 13/16 inches
Gift of the Friends of the Philadelphia Museum of Art

Rauschenberg's application of silk-screened images to canvas for the first time in the fall of 1962 brought his decade-long fascination with collage and found objects in line with the contemporary explosion of mass media. The silk-screen process allowed him to apply photographs to canvas, thereby incorporating into his paintings imagery from newspapers, art reproductions, and his own snapshots. Included in *Estate* are photographs taken from the artist's window showing the crossing of Pine and Naussau Streets as well as other New York building facades; Michelangelo's *Last Judgment* overlaid with a diagram of a clock; the Statue of Liberty; a 1962 rocket launch; a series of birds that climb up the left side of the canvas; and several repetitions of a glass of water. These images migrate variously among the group of different silk-screen paintings completed by Rauschenberg between 1962 and 1964.

Estate draws its power from the tension between the two different types of representation that he was among the first to juxtapose: photography and painting. The photographs exploit the wide variations in scale and the wealth of source material that mechanical reproduction made available, from the small and personal to the grand and public. Seemingly spontaneous splashes of paint recall the vocabulary of Abstract Expressionism while also unifying the disparate inventory of imagery on the canvas surface. In the upper right of the canvas the artist wittily emphasized the cross-fertilization of the mechanical and the hand-made, presenting a printer's color bar in freely painted blobs of pigment.

ANDY WARHOL (American, 1928–1987)

Jackie (Four Jackies) (Portraits of Mrs. Jacqueline Kennedy), 1964
Silk-screened acrylic on four canvas panels,
each 20 x 16 inches
Gift of Mrs. H. Gates Lloyd

Warhol began his "Jackie" series shortly after the assassination of John F. Kennedy in Dallas. As the basis for his paintings, he selected eight photographs from the mass-media coverage of the assassination and cropped the pictures to focus on the president's widow. The high contrast of magazine and newspaper photographs served the artist well in his process of enlarging the images and transferring them to canvas via silk screen. During 1964 Warhol produced an undocumented number of individual paintings of Jackie on canvases 20 by 16 inches, which were sold as single units and in multiple configurations. In this particular group, she is seen in four different "poses" that present a range of expressions and costumes provided by journalists' images. The view of Jackie standing with a uniformed soldier by her side, for example, crops and reverses the cover photograph from *Life* magazine on December 6, 1963.

Warhol's disavowals of artistic ingenuity have obscured the extent to which sophisticated formal choices underlay his work. A genuine media addict, he kept vast files of photojournalists' images. But he chose only an infinitesimal fraction of these to make into paintings. His selection of a photo was followed by a calculated decision on cropping; in this painting, the image that includes the half-face of a man behind Jackie reminds us that we are looking at a fragment. The color of the acrylic paint, such as the turquoise of many Jackie panels, also becomes a strongly expressive component of the final composition. Warhol's use of simple repetition is perhaps the most dramatic of all his artistic devices, as it compresses and intensifies the numbing drone of images with which we are confronted over weeks and months of newspaper, magazine, and television coverage.

JASPER JOHNS (American, born 1930)

Painted Bronze, 1960
Painted bronze, height 8 inches
Long-term loan from the artist

The title says immediately what this object is: painted bronze. The object is not, in fact, a coffee can filled with paint brushes but a sculpture. What interested Jasper Johns was "the possibility that one might take the one for the other." But, he added, "with just a little examination, it's very clear that one is not the other."[†]

Johns made his first sculpture in 1958, using an actual flashlight he coated in sculpmetal (a commercial mixture of vinyl resin and aluminum powder). After that his sculptures were entirely newly crafted, not needing the original object as an intermediary between its ordinary existence and its transformation into a work of art. To a museum viewer, the juxtaposition of a Savarin can and brushes might not appear so ordinary in the first place, but for Johns, and many painters, the old coffee can used to soak paintbrushes in turpentine was a fixture in the studio. As such, it was taken for granted, as a set of scalpels might be to a surgeon. Johns said it took him a long time to "see" it, and to see an immanent work of art.

Inspection reveals that this can and brushes are not after all the "real" thing, despite their life-size rendering. But Johns's object gains its power from more than a simple game of reality and illusion. In choosing the particular object he did, he selected one perfectly suited to explore a theme central to his virtuosity: leaps between unlike objects, between objects and works of art, between one work of art and another. Here we have an everyday intersection of coffee and paint, and a confusion between a cluster of tools and a work of art. Johns has made a sculpture with bronze but also with paint. And he has made a sculpture ostensibly about painting but really about the transformations that lie at the root of all art.

AGNES MARTIN (American, born Canada, 1912)

The Rose, 1965
Acrylic and graphite on canvas, 72 x 72 inches
Centennial gift of the Woodward Foundation

Agnes Martin has often elucidated the ideals of her art by talking about roses, the flower for which this painting is named. She has written that "When a beautiful rose dies beauty does not die because it is not really in the rose. Beauty is an awareness in the mind."[†] This statement is one measure of her belief that paintings hold the potential to suggest ephemeral but essential qualities of experience. Born in Saskatchewan, Canada, Martin came of age as a painter in Sante Fe and in New York City during the height of Abstract Expressionism, when painting promised to the viewer a direct and often emotional encounter with the sublime. Artists such as Martin were devising new ways to translate the spiritual aspirations of New York School abstraction into a more minimal and quietly expressive vocabulary. The language of the grid that Martin settled upon in 1959–60 soon became a constant in her work; it provided what she has called an "ego-less" structure to express the vision of ideal beauty that is at the core of her painting.

The six-foot-square surface of *The Rose* is painted in scumbled and textured white acrylic. Across the canvas, the artist has drawn in graphite fifteen horizontal lines intersected by seventy-two vertical lines, creating a grid of narrow rectangles. Slightly to the left of each vertical and slightly above each horizontal, she has repeated the same format in red pencil. Viewed from close up, these lines look like a series of dots made by pencils bumping across the canvas ridges. Such irregularities draw our attention to the intimacy of the artist's handwriting as it draws this rational, regular structure. Although the rose-colored pencil marks are visible only at a close distance, from afar the surface seems bathed in the palest of pink light. Most surprising is the way that the two different-colored overlapping grids, which first appear to be a flat surface pattern, generate a sensation of space behind them as well as between their different grid systems. The private experience of examining this spare and delicate picture from different distances creates a heightened awareness of how rich and transporting the experience of looking can be.

DAN FLAVIN (American, 1933–1996)

Monument to V. Tatlin, 1966
Fluorescent lights, height 147 inches
Purchased with a grant from the National
Endowment for the Arts and with funds
contributed by private donors

For Dan Flavin, the standard fluorescent light tube,
removed from its typical position and function, became a rich resource for making sculpture beginning
in 1963. Since the creation of his first fluorescent
work, dedicated to the sculptor Constantin Brancusi,
Flavin continued to name his sculptures in honor of his
artistic heroes and friends, such as Barnett Newman,
Ludwig Mies van der Rohe, and Sol LeWitt, thereby
imbuing his aesthetic project with poetic as well as
historical resonance. Named for a revolutionary-era
Russian Constructivist artist, Vladimir Tatlin, the
"Monuments to Tatlin" became Flavin's largest series,
lasting from 1964 to 1982 and encompassing not
only sculpture but also paintings, drawings, and prints.
The artist said that the publication in 1962 of Camilla
Gray's important book on the Russian avant-garde, *The
Great Experiment: Russian Art, 1863–1922,* ignited
his interest in Tatlin's *Model for a Monument to the
Third International,* a work of 1920 that is known only
from photographs. Tatlin's dynamic, spiraling steel
monument incorporated lighting and radio towers. It
was designed in celebration of the Russian revolution
and conceived in anticipation of the modern
technological age.

Flavin, who described his sculptures as "anti-
monuments," adopted materials that reflect his
ambivalent view of the utopian ideals of Tatlin's earlier
work. For this 1966 version, he used seven cool white
lights of four different standard sizes. Attached to
the wall and arranged vertically into a heraldic relief
sculpture, they are organized in a symmetrical composition according to mathematical proportions based
on their sizes. Labels for Mercury lighting products
still grace the left-hand side of every tube, emphasiz-
ing the store-bought, Readymade nature of Flavin's
materials. Displayed in the gallery, the light they
generate is familiarly harsh and tangibly concrete
but ultimately ethereal.

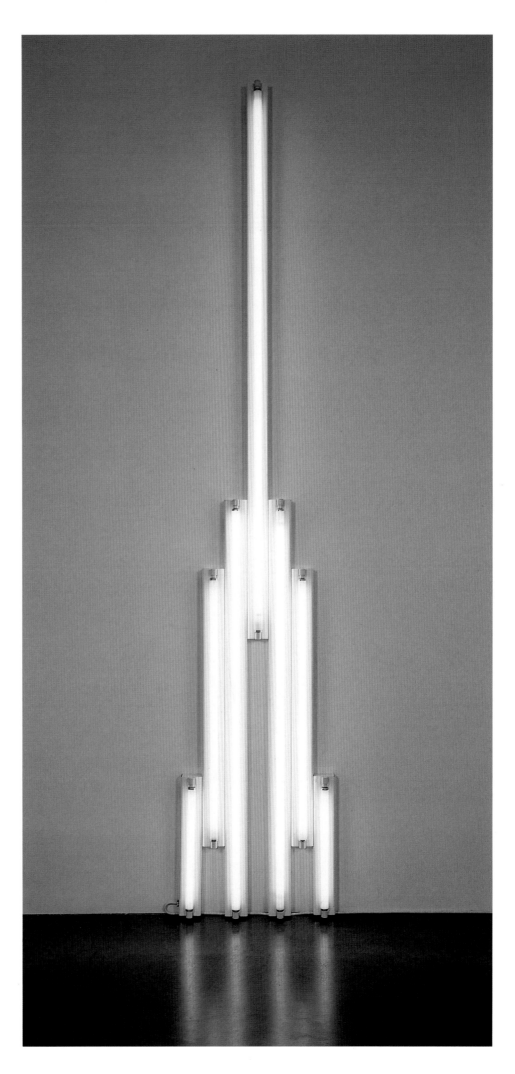

113

MARCEL BROODTHAERS (Belgian, 1924–1976)

***The Triumph of Mussels (Triomphe de Moule I
[Moules Casserole]),*** 1965
Painted and enameled iron-alloy casserole, mussel
shells partially coated with polyester resin and paint,
19¾ x 15¾ x 15¾ inches
Gift (by exchange) of Mr. and Mrs. R. Sturgis Ingersoll

The piled-up mussel shells in this piece, made in
1965, provocatively merge art with life while also iron-
ically saluting the gastronomic specialty of Broodthaers's native Belgium. The casserole pot contains a
vertiginous mass of mussel shells, held together with
a diaphanous coating of polyester resin and pigment
in colors evocative of the seashore. A former poet and
bookdealer, Broodthaers had begun his career as a
visual artist the year before, prompted by his powerful
response to American Pop art. Broodthaers
considered Pop art an extension of the work of his
hero and fellow Belgian, the Surrealist painter René
Magritte. He admired and emulated Magritte's consummate ability to elaborate a pictorial language
aimed at overturning our expectations of reality.

Broodthaers's burgeoning mussel pot also can be
understood as a meditation upon the ambiguity of language. The work turns on the pun in French between
la moule (mussel) and *le moule* (mold), and the properties of this familiar mollusk, whose shell is composed
of calcareous material secreted by the mussel, as if
sculpting its own shape. Broodthaers's description of
the casserole of surging mussel shells as an "explosion of vitality"[†] introduces an erotic reading of the
work, while his choice of medium firmly locates it
within the legacy of Marcel Duchamp.

YVES KLEIN (French, 1928–1962)

Portrait Relief I: Arman, 1962
Painted bronze on panel covered in gold leaf,
69 x 37 inches
Gift of Dr. and Mrs. William Wolgin

Many contemporary artists are associated with a
signature image or technique, but only Yves Klein laid
claim—literally gave his name—to a specific color. He
inaugurated International Klein Blue in Milan in 1957
with an exhibition of monochrome paintings. Following
the debut of I.K.B. as a painting medium, Klein employed his color blue in the service of architecture,
sculpture, murals, performance, and famously, at a
Paris gallery opening in 1958, a cocktail. His use of
blue had dual implications: the choice had profound
spiritual and poetic resonance, while at the same
time the implications of patenting a color seemed
richly ironic. The unique luminosity of I.K.B. stems
from the secret formula of clear synthetic fixative that
allows the grains of dry blue pigment to sparkle.

In the final months of his short life, Klein began a
series molding the bodies of friends and colleagues
in plaster, destined to be cast in bronze and painted
I.K.B. These portrait reliefs extended Klein's longtime
interest in using the body to make art, exemplified in
his notorious series of large paintings of the early
1960s in which he had used paint-covered women
as his "living brushes." Klein's portrait of Arman, the
French artist celebrated for his agglomerations of objects pressed into dense assemblages, is the only
portrait relief that he had time to finish. After Klein's
death, it was cast in blue-painted bronze in an edition
of six. The figure was placed against a wooden panel
gilded with gold leaf, as prescribed by the artist. The
figure of Arman was the first in what was to have been
a "Collective Portrait Relief" of several artists, including Klein himself at the center in reversed colors: gold-
covered bronze projecting from a panel of his own
International Klein Blue.

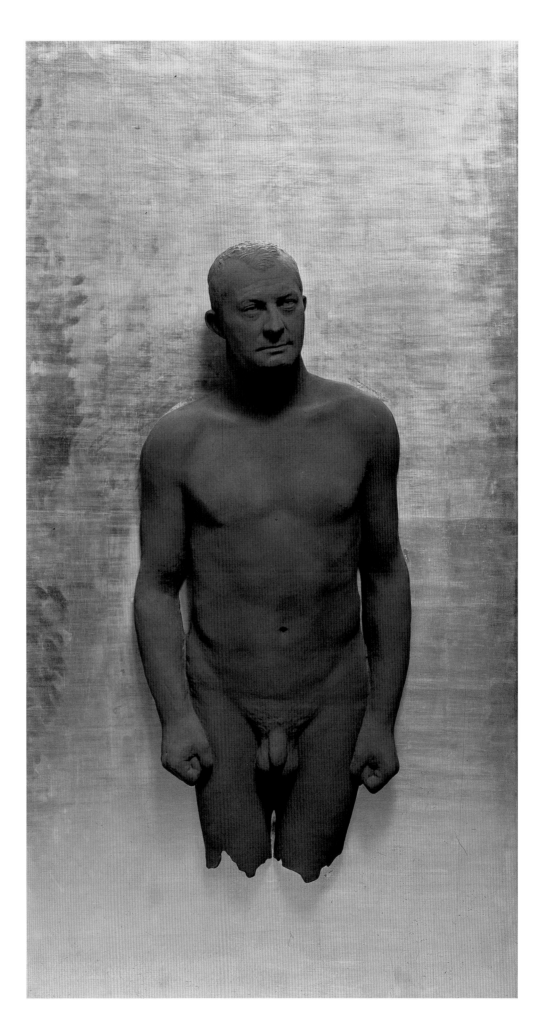

JESS (JESS COLLINS) (American, born 1923)

Ex. 6, No Traveller's Borne
(Translation No. 13), 1965
Oil on canvas on panel, 36¼ x 29¼ inches
Purchased with the Edith H. Bell Fund

The San Francisco–based artist Jess (who dropped
his surname when he decided to become an artist)
has been working on his "Translations" series since
1959. Each of these richly textured paintings is derived from an obscure source culled from the artist's
archives of old engravings, etchings, magazine illustrations, postcards, and photographs. Jess reproduces
these forgotten images in oil paintings painstakingly
built up in heavy layers of pigment to a thickness
resembling colored relief maps. Removing his source
material from its original context and transforming it
through enlargement and a palette of bubble-gum
colors, Jess completes the work by wedding the
image with a corresponding text, which he inscribes
on the back of the canvas. These paintings salvage
arcane images that modern society has discarded,
renewing their freshness and potency through the
artist's visionary imagination and meticulous
craftsmanship.

Ex. 6, No Traveller's Borne (Translation No. 13) is based
on an engraving of the earth in space by G. M. Hopkins
that appeared in the journal *Experimental Science* in
1869. In reworking the black-and-white image, Jess
employed the craggy fields of color found in the
Abstract Expressionist paintings of his teacher and
mentor, Clyfford Still. On the back, Jess inscribed
the following passage from Shakespeare's *Hamlet* to
accompany the image: "The undiscover'd Countrey,
from whose Borne / No Traveller returnes, Puzels
the will." Painted during the early years of space
travel, the picture seems to bridge the poles
of science-fiction fantasy and cosmic symbolism.

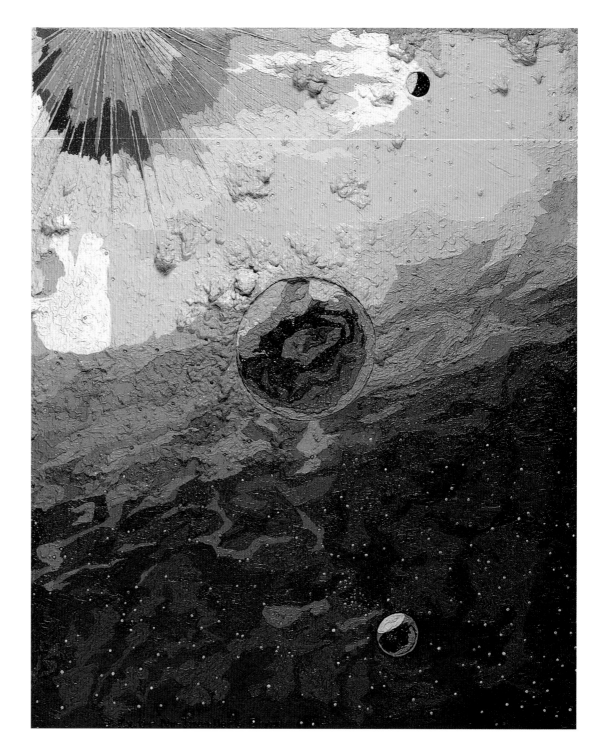

PAUL THEK (American, 1933–1988)

Meat Piece with Warhol Brillo Box, 1965
Beeswax, hair, painted wood, and Plexiglas, 14 x 17 x
17 inches
Purchased with funds contributed by the Daniel W.
Dietrich Foundation

Paul Thek takes a place in the American artistic tradition of strong individualists with distinguished predecessors ranging from Albert Pinkham Ryder to Joseph Cornell. Although he was clearly of his time and place, Thek refused to fit comfortably into a niche that shelters people who choose a creative livelihood. That sense of dislocation is nowhere more vivid than in *Meat Piece with Warhol Brillo Box*. It is from a series of works entitled as a group "Technological Reliquaries," which Thek made between 1965 and 1967 while living in New York. Thek employed a painted wood Brillo box that he obtained from Andy Warhol. He removed the top and bottom of the box, replaced them with Plexiglas, and laid the box on its side. Within, he placed a gruesomely convincing slab of bright red, fibrous flesh made of beeswax and hair.

On the surface, *Meat Piece* is a polemical statement. Thek strongly opposed what he saw as the cheerful acceptance of American consumerism expressed by Pop art, exemplified in Warhol's Brillo box. But the power of the piece goes beyond social or art criticism. Thek's alteration of the Brillo box took a secular expression of Pop into the realm of the sacred and mystical. His use of the label and format of the reliquary acknowledges the ceremony and ritual of Catholicism, which he experienced as a child and which left a permanent imprint on his work. Is the meat holy or putrid, dead or alive? (It seems to "breathe" through a small hole in the center of the glazing.) The meat's presentation in a Brillo box pointedly evokes slaughter and sickness, revealing what is normally hidden by the sanitization of daily life.

EVA HESSE (American, born Germany, 1936–1970)

Tori, 1969
Fiberglass and resin on wire mesh, largest unit
47 x 17 x 15 inches
Purchased with funds contributed by Mr. and
Mrs. Leonard Korman, Mr. and Mrs. Keith Sachs,
Marion Boulton Stroud, Frances and Bayard T.
Storey, and other Museum funds

Eva Hesse belonged to a loosely associated group
of New York artists who, at the end of the 1960s,
rebelled against the strict geometry and cool materiality of Minimalism and began making art that came
to be known under the rubric "antiform" or "process
art." The arrangement and orientation of their sculptures often were unfixed and were characterized by

experimentation with fluid, flexible materials such
as latex and fiberglass.

Tori consists of nine podlike forms of varying size.
Hesse chose as her title the plural of the word "torus,"
derived from the Latin word for "protuberance." The
word has various anatomical, botanical, geometric,
and architectural meanings, but all refer to a rounded,
swelling form. The armature of each pod is made
of wire mesh screen, loosely wrapped and pinned
together at the top and bottom but spread open in
the middle, as if the pod had burst apart. Hesse
coated the surfaces with fiberglass and resin, a
mixture that is not entirely compatible with the wire
mesh below, and the mottled skin still manifests the
difficulty with which it was applied. The present configuration of the nine elements echoes photographs of

the work in Hesse's studio, its apparently casual
arrangement looking more like something discovered
by chance than deliberately set in place.

Hesse's career as a sculptor of groundbreaking work
lasted little more than five years, ending abruptly
with her death from a brain tumor in 1970. Inevitably,
the tragedy of her short life has been superimposed
on the readings of her fragile sculptures. But the
eloquence of *Tori* transcends a biographical reading,
bearing witness to the universal human condition of
profound vulnerability.

ROBERT SMITHSON (American, 1938–1973)

Red Sandstone Corner Piece, 1968
Mirrors and sandstone, 48 x 48 inches
Purchased (by exchange) for the Samuel S. White 3rd
and Vera White Collection and with funds contributed
by Henry S. McNeil, Jr., Ella B. Schaap, Marion
Boulton Stroud, and Mr. and Mrs. Harvey Gushner

Red Sandstone Corner Piece takes its place among
Smithson's conceptual mappings of the terrain of
his native New Jersey, an area he found replete with
physical, historical, and scientific resonance. Focused
on the dialogue between an actual site in the industrial
landscape and the neutral space of the art gallery or
museum, his thinking reached an apotheosis in the

essay "The Monuments of Passaic," published in 1967,
one year before he made this piece. Assuming the
outlook of a historian or a geologist from the future
looking back on a dying civilization, Smithson offered
a guided tour of a postwar industrial wasteland punc-
tuated by structures such as pumping derricks or
pipes and drainage facilities. This concern with places
that blur the boundaries between nature and culture
informed the making of this sculpture, as Smithson
charted a new path within the venerable tradition of
sculptors seeking stone from quarries to carve
their work.

Reinventing this narrative, Smithson took a trip—what
he called an "anti-expedition"—to an "uncelebrated"
place in New Jersey: Red Sand Hook Quarry. *Red

Sandstone Corner Piece,* created by piling a sample
of deep red rocks in a corner made by three 4-foot-
square mirrors, is the only sculpture that resulted from
this excursion. Fragmented, modest, and without the
volume or coherence typically associated with three-
dimensional sculpture, these remains of Smithson's
journey make for a piece as lacking in monumentality
as the expired site itself. Although the strong contrast
between the warm-colored earth and the cool geometry of mirrors is undeniable, the questions raised by
Smithson's unconventional sculpture point in two directions at once, toward the physical space of the gallery
and the outdoors, while also challenging the assump-
tion that there is a fixed ordering to their relationship.

ROY LICHTENSTEIN (American, 1923–1997)

Still Life with Goldfish, 1974
Oil and Magna on canvas, 80 x 60 inches
Purchased with the Edith H. Bell Fund

Lichtenstein is best known for importing the vocabulary of comic strips and commercial advertising into the more exalted realm of oil painting on canvas, an art christened "Pop" when it made its debut in the early 1960s. However, Lichtenstein did not limit his foraging to the world of vernacular imagery but became an agile and dedicated trafficker in the history of art. *Still Life with Goldfish* belongs to a series of still-life paintings he made between 1972 and 1974 that take as the point of departure the work of Henri Matisse.

This canvas offers an interpretation of a painting close at hand to Lichtenstein: Matisse's *Goldfish,* of 1914–15, in the collection of the Museum of Modern Art, New York. Matisse seems to have discovered for Western art the intriguing motif of the goldfish bowl, and since then it has become singularly identified with him and a favorite object of Lichtenstein's appropriations. From Matisse's painting, Lichtenstein borrowed the central element of the cylindrical bowl holding two swimming red fish, placed atop a small table. He also repeated the fruit beside it and the scrolled grillwork of the balcony beyond the open window. Extending Matisse's penchant for inserting images of his previous paintings into new ones, Lichtenstein has slyly slipped in a drawing of a woman by Matisse completely unrelated to *Goldfish.* However, Lichtenstein's painting eschews the sensuous color and texture of Matisse's surfaces and the moodiness of Matisse's hesitations and reworkings. The slick surface of Lichtenstein's smooth acrylic paint and the flat sections of unmixed colors produce an image that is wholly confident and clear.

CLAES OLDENBURG (American, born Sweden, 1929)

Giant Three-Way Electric Plug (Scale B), 1970
Cherry wood, height 58 inches
Purchased with the Fiske Kimball Fund and with
funds contributed by the Daniel W. Dietrich Foundation,
Mr. and Mrs. David N. Pincus, Dr. and Mrs. William
Wolgin, and anonymous donors

The image of the three-way electrical plug first
appeared in Oldenburg's work in 1965, in an
Expressionistic charcoal and wash drawing that
made the object look like a dripping popsicle on two
sticks. Oldenburg constructed a large three-dimensional cardboard version in the same year, which he
suspended to make the plug seem light and airy, like
a kite or a balloon. This piece was crushed when a
workman fell on it at the 1968 Documenta, the presti-
gious international exposition held in Kassel, Germany,
and it was returned to the artist's studio for repair. In
rebuilding the cardboard plug, Oldenburg became
interested in the subject again and produced a number
of other versions in materials including Cor-Ten steel,
canvas, mahogany, and cherry wood. The original
three-way plug that the artist worked from to make
these sculptures was a standard American design
made of Bakelite, which he magnified to a gigantic
scale so that the plug took on a formal affinity with
architecture.

Oldenburg first gained notoriety in the early 1960s
when he opened a small storefront on New York's
Lower East Side called The Store, where he blurred
the distinction between art and commerce by selling
painted replicas of food and other everyday com-
modities. Unwary customers found hamburgers and
dresses fabricated out of hard plaster and rendered
in a paint-spattered parody of Abstract Expressionism.
The artist's subsequent enlargements of familiar
domestic appliances, household furniture, and other
consumer products often point to the fetishistic potential of common objects in a witty or erotic way. The
inflated scale of these works unleashed a wealth of
metaphorical associations for Oldenburg, who has
spoken of the rounded, geometric shape of the *Giant
Three-Way Electric Plug* in terms of a skull, a cannon,
an anchor, a nut, Mickey Mouse, and even the Hagia
Sophia mosque in Istanbul, Turkey.

SIDNEY GOODMAN (American, born 1936)

Figures in a Landscape, 1972–73
Oil on canvas, 55 x 96 inches
Purchased with the Philadelphia Foundation Fund
(by exchange) and the Adele Haas Turner and
Beatrice Pastorius Turner Memorial Fund

A powerful silence reigns in the paintings of Sidney
Goodman, paintings packed with the drama of what is
left unsaid. His work is steeped in the perfectionism
that is part of Philadelphia's grand figurative tradition,
developed over the course of previous centuries by
such masters as Charles Willson Peale and Thomas
Eakins. But Goodman has directed his powers of
observation and verisimilitude to uniquely expressive

and metaphorical ends, singularly relevant to his
own time and place. Rarely looking beyond his own
family and friends, neighborhood, or the newspaper
for inspiration for figures and settings, the artist
has found the basic ordinariness of his subject
matter integral to the air of disquiet produced by
his paintings.

Although the title of the work gives no such indication,
this painting is a portrait of Goodman's family. The
artist's intimacy with his sitters is nowhere in evidence,
as they occupy distinct portions of the monumental
canvas, absorbed in their wholly separate mental and
physical spaces. The dark shadows slicing the landscape and the ominous clouds gathering overhead
provide an unambiguously foreboding mood. Goodman's

paintings bring to light the grotesque element of the
everyday furnishings of people's lives. Here, for example, the thick red rubber Hippity Hop toy that was a
ubiquitous element of American childhood in the late
1960s and early 1970s becomes a monstrous adjunct
to the little girl sitting on it, virtually attached to her as
its red joins the white and blue of her clothing. Goodman adamantly denies that his paintings are designed
to communicate a specific message. It is nonetheless
difficult to contemplate this family without finding within
it the full spectrum of sociopolitical traumas that
pummeled the American psyche in the early 1970s.

GEORGE SEGAL (American, born 1924)

Exit, 1975
Plaster, wood, plastic, metal, and electric light,
84 x 72 x 36 inches
Gift of the Friends of the Philadelphia Museum of Art

In 1961 George Segal, who had trained as a painter, invented a process of creating direct casts of the human body with common surgical bandages dipped in plaster and water, materials typically used by doctors to set broken limbs. His discovery signaled a definitive break with the activity of painting on canvas. For Segal, sculpture opened the door to the exploration of human psychology and the expression of human dramas, concerns that informed his training as a painter in an atmosphere dominated by Abstract Expressionism. As he said, "Casting left me free to compose and to present content. I could report on my model and not on me; it was a rejection of the psychological distance of the canvas painter."[†]

Segal discovered new narrative possibilities for his ghostly white life-size human surrogates when he began situating them in evocative environments constructed from real objects, such as furniture and appliances. These assemblage techniques, joined with the concerns of narrative and abstraction, are explored in *Exit*. The model for this sculpture was a young assistant at the Sidney Janis Gallery in New York, where Segal's work first attracted attention when he participated in the 1962 exhibition "New Realism," the show that launched Pop art. The figure of the walking woman is one element in the collage-like tableau that Segal created from squares of different dimensions, materials, colors, and letters. Sandwiched between two parallel planes, one of perforated metal and the other a lightboard suggestive of a glowing abstract painting, she is captured in a moment that is both banal and profound. The word "Exit" makes an ambiguous comment on the quiet existential drama, as the figure passes from one undefined space to another.

EDNA ANDRADE (American, born 1917)

Night Sea, 1977
Acrylic on canvas, 72 x 71¹⁵⁄₁₆ inches
Gift of the Philadelphia Arts Exchange

The composition and visual effects of *Night Sea* reflect the remarkable balance of rationality and intuition that informs Edna Andrade's approach to painting. Created from simple straight lines of iridescent green and pink on a rich blue-black ground, the rhythmic, wavelike image is at once solidly geometric and precise as well as constantly in flux. Seemingly without beginning or end, the painting changes, depending on where the eye and mind focus. Straight lines curve, colors emit different intensities of light, and inescapably flat elements bend, project, and bulge into space.

Every line of *Night Sea* seems to connect to every other line and then to change color and direction at sharp angles, either splayed out to produce a generous curve or concentrated into dense knots of color, light, and energy.

An influential artist and teacher who has lived and worked in Philadelphia since 1946, Andrade first explored optical phenomena in her painting in the 1960s, when she was presenting courses on color and design at the Philadelphia College of Art. The clarity of her conception and the sureness of her drawing also reflect her work in the 1940s as an architectural draftsman for government projects. *Night Sea* belongs to a group of works from the 1970s painted with a limited palette of bright colors finely drawn on dark grounds in which she devised

mathematical systems to generate elegant, curving surface patterns and surprising visual effects using straight lines. The rules she used are only intermittently revealed by close observation; more prominent are the organic unity of the whole, the delicacy of the line, and the interdependent relationship of drawing, volume, color, and light that *Night Sea* projects. Its colors and fluctuating waves recall the effects of phosphorescence in the ocean glowing on a dark night, joining principles of science and wave theory with her inspired imagination to determine the ordered principles that structure her painting.

RICHARD DIEBENKORN (American, 1922–1993)

Ocean Park No. 79, 1975
Oil on canvas, 93 x 81 inches
Purchased with a grant from the National
Endowment for the Arts and with funds
contributed by private donors

Diebenkorn's "Ocean Park" series of eloquent abstractions represents the artist's response to the intoxicating sunlight and the expansive landscape of Southern California, as well as to the luminous palettes of Matisse and Bonnard. It takes its name from a section of Santa Monica, a seaside town on the edge of Los Angeles, where the artist had a studio overlooking the Pacific Ocean. Diebenkorn began the series in 1967

and worked on it until 1988, producing more than 140 subtle and playful variations. This painting, number 79 in the series, is a supreme example of the artist's fascination with the Pacific coastline's long, uninterrupted planes of sea and air and beach and freeway. The composition is built with the aid of a scaffold of ruled lines that divides the canvas into a series of vertical and horizontal rectangles traversed by sharp diagonals. Diebenkorn daringly summarized the beachfront landscape by reducing it to a gridlike system of abutting and interlocking color planes. Painted in soft, bleached colors scraped down to produce a translucent surface, the overlapping bands of deep blue, turquoise, and yellow strongly evoke the seashore as seen from a distance, perhaps through a window.

The artist emphasized painstaking construction and process in the "Ocean Park" series. A close examination of the multilayered paint surface of *Ocean Park No. 79* reveals numerous changes and corrections, erasures and emendations. The ghosts of earlier layers of pigment, accidental drips, and submerged charcoal drawing shine through the thin veils of overpainting. The cumulative effect of these revisions in Diebenkorn's work suggests the ritual of a daily journal. Infused with the marine light of California, his is an art of duration that requires long and thoughtful viewing.

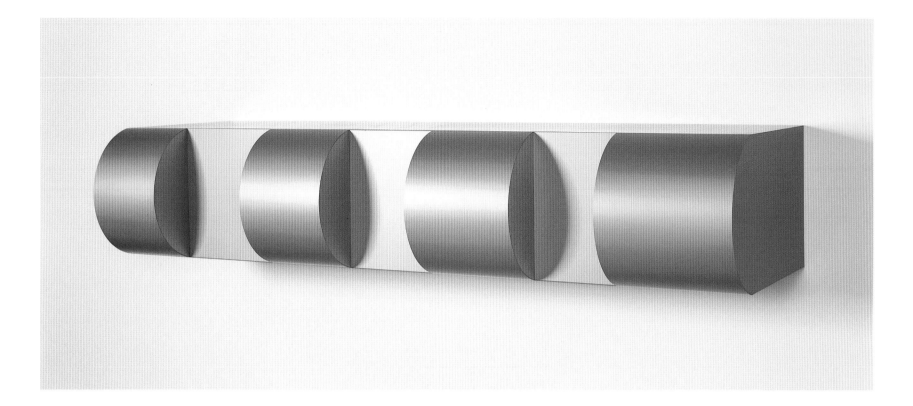

DONALD JUDD (American, 1928–1994)

Untitled, 1974
Anodized aluminum, 25 x 76 x 14 inches
Gift (by exchange) of Mr. and Mrs. R. Sturgis Ingersoll

One of the most important thinkers and artists of his generation, Donald Judd began writing criticism and making art only a few years after Jackson Pollock's death in 1956, but he wholly rejected one of the fundamental tenets of Pollock's generation: the idea of a necessary connection between the inner psychology of the creator and the appearance or meaning of his art. Judd first sought to eliminate these assumptions when, in 1964, he began to have his work industrially fabricated, based on his drawings. This technique created taut, anonymous-looking structures characterized by unity of color, image, surface, and shape; technology allowed him to eradicate any trace of his own hand. Calling his works "specific objects," Judd emphasized his intention to create concrete physical things that did not partake of the illusionary space occupied by either painting or sculpture, categories he relegated to the past.

This 1974 piece belongs to a group of works he described as "bull-nosed." The nickname describes the shape of a particular type of chisel, and Judd was undoubtedly pleased by the analogy between his work and a practical tool. The eccentric shape of this relief sculpture that projects from the wall is the result of a mathematical formula, combining rectangular and semispherical elements into a seamless, geometrical whole. Its projecting volumes and negative spaces progress horizontally in dimensions that are inversely related to one another, but when seen from its short end, it presents a simple silhouette. The complexity of Judd's work and thought extends to his adoption of gorgeously rich colors. The magnificent chartreuse gives the object an opulent intensity in dramatic contrast to the severity of its shape. The aluminum itself was colored during fabrication, like a piece of machinery. Judd's chosen palette also adds a Pop art twist and space-age glitz to what the artist defined as a conceptually demanding and visually austere aesthetic.

SOL LeWITT (American, born 1928)

On a Blue Ceiling, Eight Geometric Figures:
Circle, Trapezoid, Parallelogram, Rectangle,
Square, Triangle, Right Triangle, X
(Wall Drawing No. 351), 1981
Chalk and latex paint on plaster,
15 feet 6 inches x 54 feet 7 inches
Purchased with a grant from the National Endowment
for the Arts and with funds contributed by Mrs. H. Gates
Lloyd, Mr. and Mrs. N. Richard Miller, Mrs. Donald A.
Petrie, Eileen and Peter Rosenau, Ella B. Schaap,
Frances and Bayard T. Storey, Marion Boulton Stroud,
and two anonymous donors (by exchange), with addi-
tional funds from Dr. and Mrs. William Wolgin, the
Daniel W. Dietrich Foundation, and the Friends of
the Philadelphia Museum of Art

This wall drawing is described fully by its title, although
the words give no clue to the work's joyful presence.
Designed by Sol LeWitt in April 1981 specifically for
the gallery it occupies, the work was produced by a
group of LeWitt's assistants and Museum staff members. The following year the Philadelphia Museum of
Art purchased the wall drawing, which means simply
that the Museum owns the idea and the right to exe-
cute it or to erase it and to allow others to do so, as
expressed in a certificate signed by the artist.

LeWitt made his first wall drawing at the Paula Cooper
Gallery in New York in autumn 1968. His invention was
one of many radical artistic assertions that coincided
with a cataclysmic art historical moment. It was an art
resolutely opposed to the commercialism surrounding
painting and sculpture, distrustful of the aesthetic value
of permanence, and allied more closely to philosophy
or science than to decor. LeWitt's early wall drawings
were done in thin graphite lines that subtly but authori-
tatively altered surfaces. Over the decades, as his work
gradually abandoned the need to present a restrained
appearance in order to prove its intellectual basis, his
wall drawings have evolved into lively, lush painted
designs of bold shapes and colors.

LeWitt's revolution was manifold, transforming modern
drawing from a small-scale format subservient to painting or sculpture into something grandly autonomous.
Perhaps most radical was LeWitt's disassociation of
the creation of an idea from the execution of a work
of art: while the instructions are indisputably his, the
manufacture need not be and usually is not. As the
artist points out, the wall drawings, like music, will be
done differently by every interpreter. Despite LeWitt's
specified prescriptions (how many coats and what
brand of paint, for example), *On a Blue Ceiling* draws
its strength from the individual spirits and hands of
its team of makers.

JONATHAN BOROFSKY (American, born 1942)

2,841,777 Sing, 1978–83
Acrylic on canvas, three Polaroid prints, painted
aluminum, and stereo cassette with a tape loop,
127 x 96 inches
Purchased with the Edward and Althea Budd Fund,
the Adele Haas Turner and Beatrice Pastorius Turner
Memorial Fund, and funds contributed by Marion
Boulton Stroud, Mr. and Mrs. Harvey Gushner, Ella B.
Schaap, Mrs. H. Gates Lloyd, Eileen and Peter
Rosenau, Frances and Bayard T. Storey, Dr. and Mrs.
William Wolgin, Mrs. Donald A. Petrie, Mark Rosenthal,
Harold P. Starr, and two anonymous donors

Like much of Borofsky's work, *Sing* is a self-sufficient
work of art that first served as one component of a
large extravaganza. It originated as part of a presentation at the Paula Cooper Gallery in New York in 1983
and was reincarnated in a retrospective exhibition
at the Philadelphia Museum of Art the following year.
Both installations were circuslike, densely packed
with sculptures, and filled with a chorus of sounds.
Borofsky is a master of the art form known as "installation" or "environment," treating a given gallery or
museum space as a surrogate studio in order to
re-create the chaos of his usual work setting.

Sing presents an exuberantly fanciful image of the
artist. Dressed in a blue robe, he receives a tablet
from above, much as Moses received the Ten Com-
mandments, caught in an explosive swirl of paint that
suggests the force of divine presence. This painting
cannot be contained in two dimensions: applied to its
surface are Polaroid snapshots of the artist's hands
and foot, and springing from its top edge is a huge
aluminum ribbon in the form of a human profile,
mouth open in song. Indeed, the artist has obeyed
the command printed on the tablet and attached to
the painting a tape recording of his own singing.

The full title of the work, *2,841,777 Sing,* reflects
Borofsky's habit of signing each work he makes with a
number. Borofsky began his career as a painter and
sculptor but abandoned art-making in the late 1960s
and turned to the meditative activity of writing number
charts on sheets of paper. As he eventually began to
make objects again, he continued the counting, attach-
ing numbers to individual pieces. Marking time and
work, the numbers provide an existential dimension to
Borofsky's joyous enterprise.

THOMAS CHIMES (American, born 1921)

Portrait of Alfred Jarry, 1974
Oil on panel, 12 x 11¹¹⁄₁₆ inches
Purchased with the Adele Haas Turner and Beatrice
Pastorius Turner Memorial Fund

Portrait of Apollinaire, 1974
Oil on panel, 12 x 9³⁄₈ inches
Purchased with the Adele Haas Turner and Beatrice
Pastorius Turner Memorial Fund

Portrait of Antonin Artaud, 1974
Oil on panel, 9¹⁄₈ x 9¹⁄₈ inches
Gift of the artist

These paintings belong to a series of forty-eight portraits that Chimes painted between 1973 and 1978
of writers, inventors, and philosophers. The three
paintings salute significant figures in the French theater. The writer Alfred Jarry (1873–1907) appears
several times in the series. Chiefly known today as the
creator of the anarchic play *Ubu Roi (King Ubu),* Jarry
provoked a riot in 1896 when his play opened in Paris
and ushered in the modern era of theater. Chimes
based his image of Jarry on a photograph taken by
Nadar at the height of the *Ubu Roi* scandal. The picture shows Jarry with his distinctive mane of shoulder-
length dark hair, oval face, and piercing black eyes.
The artist cropped the image to focus on the brooding
visage of the playwright, then twenty-three years old.

The portrait of Apollinaire (1880–1918) depicts the
avant-garde poet and playwright shortly before the
premiere of his farcical play *Les Mamelles de Tirésias
(The Breasts of Tirésias)* in 1917. He wears the uni-
form of the French army, from which he received a
medical discharge after suffering a serious head
wound. The portrait of Antonin Artaud (1896–1948)
shows the artist, writer, and theatrical innovator as he
looked in 1920, still profoundly traumatized by the
horrors of World War I. Artaud's mental stability was
severely impaired by military service, and Chimes's
depiction of his rolling eyes and severe facial features captures his tortured sensibility. In 1926 Artaud
cofounded the Alfred Jarry Theatre in Paris, where
he revived the extreme tactics and shocking icono-
clasm of the *Ubu* plays.

Chimes's haunting series of portraits reveals his
strong feelings of affinity and continuity with his beloved hero, Alfred Jarry, and others who have followed
in his footsteps. Each intimate sepia-toned image,
reminiscent of a nineteenth-century daguerreotype,
is enshrined within a crafted, oversized wooden frame
that situates the work between a family snapshot
and an icon.

ELLSWORTH KELLY (American, born 1923)

Diagonal with Curve III, 1978
Oil on canvas, 135 x 99 inches
Gift of the Friends of the Philadelphia Museum of Art

Ellsworth Kelly's decisive transformation of line, shape, and color into works that occupy the territory shared by painting, sculpture, and architecture is powerfully evident in *Diagonal with Curve III,* one of a series of five monochrome paintings that explores the tension between straight lines and curves. Kelly has remarked that the experience of seeing a small group of Juan Gris's paintings at the Philadelphia Museum of Art in the 1950s first led him to conceive of paintings in series that could be thought of as a related whole, especially when exhibited together. His exploration of the expressive potential of simple curved lines and shapes derives from the same period, specifically from his 1952 proposal for a book to be called "Line Form and Plane," which included an elegant linear drawing of a curve isolated against a stark ground.

In making a canvas curve, Kelly defied the orthogonal organization of parallel lines and planes that has for centuries been the framework for painting. He undid many assumptions about the physical reality, conceptual boundaries, and function of pictures on walls. Taking abstraction to a level of simplicity that would have been unthinkable to Constantin Brancusi or Jean Arp—early modern artists from whom Kelly took inspiration—*Diagonal with Curve III* unsettles definitions of what is painting and what is architecture, as well as what is figure and what is ground. The two parallel edges at the right and left of the canvas establish a contrast with the differently bowed longer sides of the work, with their edges meeting at masterfully orchestrated angles. Using remarkably restricted means, Kelly drew with color and edge—an approach that evokes Henri Matisse's cut-outs—to charge the black matte painted surface with an electrifying energy and to create a soaring, monumental presence.

WILLEM De KOONING (American, born Netherlands, 1904–1997)

Untitled XXI, 1982
Oil on canvas, 77 x 88 inches
Partial and promised gift of Gisela and Dennis Alter

De Kooning, who came of age in the 1940s and 1950s during the efflorescence of Abstract Expressionism, was the only original member of the group to continue to extend the basic stylistic premises of gestural painting long after the movement itself had waned. When he was nearly eighty years old, de Kooning's work took the path of many "old masters," whether modern or traditional, settling into a

recognizably distinct late style. Characterized by a reduced number of colors and textures that vary from the smoothly sanded to the sensuously brushed, *Untitled XXI* suggests the clarity, purity, and intensity of de Kooning's final body of work while demonstrating his persistent yet subtle swerving between the figural and the abstract.

De Kooning's usual method in the 1980s was to generate pictures from earlier pictures using charcoal and tracing paper, sometimes making monoprints from works in progress to commence a new work. *Untitled XXI* therefore records many exchanges between the artist's hand, brush, and canvas and is also a bravura demonstration of de Kooning's visceral

understanding of the density, reflectivity, and texture of oil paint, qualities he continuously explored throughout his long career. Ribbonlike spreads of blue paint dance on a surface built up from white paint, which is scraped and sanded in areas. Accents of bright red, hinting at lips or flesh, fold through the complicated pictorial space, often with abrupt changes of direction. Complex surface variations are created by the ghostlike residue of paint that has been partially removed and the shadowy presence of the brush grazing the surface. What is at once dramatic and erotic is the language of paint itself with de Kooning's energetic facility in adjusting space, line, color, and texture to engage the viewer's eye and emotions.

FRANCESCO CLEMENTE (Italian, born 1952)

Hunger, 1980
Gouache on Pondicherry paper, joined by
cotton strips, 93¹/₂ x 96¹/₂ inches
Promised gift of Marion Boulton Stroud

The ritualistic and sensual imagery of ancient India and
the living tradition of its centuries-old artistic
techniques have inspired the Italian-born artist
Francesco Clemente since his first visit to the country
in 1973. One of a series of large-scale gouache
paintings, *Hunger* was completed following the artist's
extended stay in Madras in 1978 and 1979, when
he became immersed in Indian philosophies and in the
crafts of local artisans. *Hunger* uses the handmade
paper produced in Pondicherry, a village south of
Madras. Twelve individual pages are joined together
to create the ground for this large-scale painting. Its
format suggests a book taken apart and reassembled,
and it also retains the delicacy and intimacy of Indian
miniature painting. However, the artist has adapted
the watercolor medium to an expansive scale to
create a contemporary painting about the primal
theme of desire.

In Clemente's characteristically subtle marriage of
Eastern and Western traditions, the snake consuming
its own tail—an ancient symbol of eternity—assumes
the shape of a vast circular form and stretches across
the grid pattern made by the individual sheets of paper.
Painterly and luminous, the blue, purple, and green
wash creates a nonspecific, atmospheric landscape
setting for the event depicted in the lower corner of
the picture: a ravenous man making a meal of the
creature, balancing a portion of the large snake in a
ceramic bowl. His bared teeth draw blood, and his
greedy expression reflects the insatiability of his appe-
tite. The energy mobilized to consume the apparently
endless snake, noticeable in the man's arms and grip
as well as in his extended fingers, has toppled a glass
of water. Its wasted, spilling contents suggest the
limitations of gratification.

CY TWOMBLY (American, born 1928)

Fifty Days at Iliam, 1977–78
Oil, oil crayon, and graphite on ten canvases,
largest canvas 118 x 193½ inches
Gift (by exchange) of Samuel S. White 3rd and
Vera White

Cy Twombly has chosen to spend much of his life in
Italy and to ground his art in the history of Western
culture rather than the imagery of contemporary America. In *Fifty Days at Iliam,* Twombly addressed a defin-
ing work of classical literature: Homer's *Iliad,* the epic
recitation of the final fifty days of the Trojan War, probably written before 700 B.C. Undertaking a project of

unprecedented scope in his work, Twombly created
his own interpretation of Homer's narrative in a monumental ten-part painting. He relied on the sensuous
visual language he had developed over the past
twenty-five years, full of scrawling marks, clumps of
paint straight from the tube, drips, erasures, and
legible numbers and letters. His vocabulary ranges
from lushly erotic organic shapes to hieroglyphics
of nearly invisible subtlety.

Twombly stipulated the spatial configuration of the ten
large canvases in a presentation that was sequential
as well as logical thematically. An antechamber
contains the emblematic painting *Shield of Achilles,*
the armor made for the Greek warrior by the gods,

with energy forces drawn from the four corners of the
universe. Nine paintings in the adjoining gallery
present the chronological unfolding of the story,
progressing from the scene of Achilles' pivotal
decision to join the fight against Troy (Iliam) to an
almost blank canvas imbued with the silence of death.
Twombly designed the installation so that the four
paintings on one side of the room present a
predominantly Greek mood, passionate and explosive,
while the four across from them embody the Trojan
character, contemplative and cool. Presiding over the
gallery from the far wall is the monumental *Shades of
Achilles, Patroclus, and Hector,* an elegiac salute to
the three fallen heroes of the war.

ELIZABETH MURRAY (American, born 1940)

Just in Time, 1981
Oil on two canvas sections, 106½ x 97 inches overall
Purchased with the Edward and Althea Budd Fund, the
Adele Haas Turner and Beatrice Pastorius Turner
Memorial Fund, and funds contributed by Marion
Boulton Stroud and Lorine E. Vogt

The transformation of real objects painted in combinations of unexpected colors on irregular shaped
canvases has been Murray's recognizable terrain since
the late 1970s. The artist's exuberant, often humorous, paintings take as their theme the mundane
objects of daily life, allowing her to navigate an idiosyncratic line between domesticity and abstraction.
Her psychologically charged vocabulary of enlarged
and fractured motifs includes shoes, coffee cups,
paintbrushes, tables, and chairs. Murray's amalgam
of painting and sculpture can be compared to the
work of Frank Stella and Ellsworth Kelly, although
her antecedents also extend to the still lifes of Paul
Cézanne and Juan Gris, among others.

In *Just in Time,* two parts of a giant cup and saucer
seem to hover at that point of magnetic tension between snapping together and pulling apart. The jagged
breaks in the crockery suggest conflict, but the two
separate canvases are linked in a unified whole by the
artist's sensual use of color and bold, simplified imagery. The cup is a recurring image for Murray and she
has spoken of her fascination with the formal and emotional properties of the drinking vessels depicted in
her work. The artist's early admiration for Walt Disney
is clear in the wonderful representation of steam, rendered in bright pink, which rises from the coffee cup
like a cloud. Murray imbues this humble household
object with a monumentality that reveals the metaphorical possibilities of everyday things. After all,
according to Murray, "that's what art is. Art is an
epiphany in a coffee cup."[†]

FRANK STELLA (American, born 1936)

Hockenheim, 1982
Oil stick, urethane enamel, fluorescent alkyd, and
Magna on etched magnesium, 124 x 128 x 19 inches
Purchased with funds contributed by Muriel and
Philip Berman and gift (by exchange) of the
Woodward Foundation

Hockenheim is named after the famous motor-racing
track south of Frankfurt that hosts the annual German
Grand Prix. Frank Stella's long-standing infatuation with
racing cars first surfaced in his work in 1960, when
he named an abstract painting after a Spanish Ferrari
driver who was killed in a race three years earlier. In

1976 the German automobile company BMW commissioned Stella to design a paint job for one of its
racing cars. The artist's passionate involvement in this
project led to several trips to Europe to see the major
races there. The competitive excitement and high
degree of risk involved in Formula 1 motor racing inspired Stella, who recognized the aesthetic possibilities of the hairpin turns and twisting chicanes for his
own metal reliefs. The artist began his "Circuit" series
in 1980 and, over the next four years, produced a
large number of elaborate, painted constructions
named after international racetracks.

Hockenheim plays with the question of how far one
can extend a painting from the wall without turning it

into sculpture. The magnesium support was
constructed in a factory according to Stella's instructions, which called for extravagant, serpentine shapes
such as arabesques, curlicues, and curvilinear forms
resembling G clefs to be cut from sheets of metal.
Welded and bolted together, these shapes create a
dense jungle of interweaving, multilayered forms that
tease the viewer's perception of depth through subtle
interplays of positive and negative space. Once the
completed structure arrived in his studio, Stella used a
wide range of materials and techniques to enliven the
factory-fresh surfaces with exuberant, neonlike hues.
Stella's careening line and breakneck shifts in color
evoke the vitality of high-speed racing cars and the
sinuous turns of a racetrack.

GERHARD RICHTER (German, born 1932)

180 Colors (180 Farben), 1971
Enamel paint on canvas, 78½ x 78½ inches
Gift (by exchange) of Mrs. Herbert Cameron Morris

180 Colors is one of a set of four multicolored paintings, each bearing the same title, that Richter showed
at the 1972 Documenta, the international art exhibition
held in Kassel, Germany. The artist began his investigations into the complex permutations of color charts
in 1966, with a small painting entitled *10 Colors*. That
work was produced in reaction to Pop art, in particular
the paintings of Andy Warhol and Roy Lichtenstein,
who enthusiastically adopted commercial techniques
and subject matter drawn from consumer culture.
The subsequent series of paintings was based on
the color charts that are shown to customers by paint
suppliers to help them choose the colors they want
for their home. Richter transformed the handy-sized,
industrially manufactured paint swatches into huge
tableaux as a way of exploring the potentials and
limits of painting, linking his work with the concerns
of Conceptual art and Minimalism.

In *180 Colors*, Richter confronts us with a composition
made up of 180 blocks of color. Each rectangle has
an even coat of glossy enamel and is framed within
the white grid of the bare canvas, which resembles an
enlarged page from a paint sample book. Inspired by
the formulas used by paint suppliers to mix any
number of colors, the artist used a mathematical
equation to create his picture. Richter twice mixed the
three primary colors—red, yellow, and blue—to get
12 hues (3 x 2 x 2 = 12). Then, from each of those
12 hues, he mixed 15 varying tones from light to dark
to make 180 colors (12 x 15 = 180). The mathematical precision with which the colors were mixed
contrasts with Richter's coincidental arrangement of
the color patches. The arbitrary juxtaposition of colors
coalesces in the same way that a random selection of
numbers will line up to win a game of bingo. As Richter
explained: "Colours match the same way as the right
bingo numbers will. . . . Any sequence of numbers is
always right and credible if it is the correct one."[†]

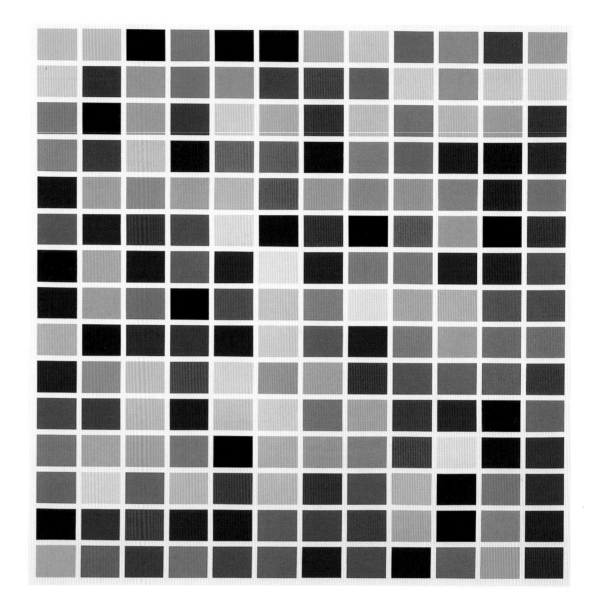

ANDY WARHOL (American, 1928–1987)

Camouflage Self-Portrait, 1986
Synthetic polymer paint and silk screen on canvas,
82 x 82 inches
Acquired with funds contributed by the Committee
on Twentieth-Century Art and as a partial gift of the
Andy Warhol Foundation for the Visual Arts, Inc.

Andy Warhol's self-portrait is best seen in relationship
to the artist's role as a keen observer of contemporary American society in pursuit of celebrity and of the
ways its images come to define reality. Famous for his
paradoxical mix of elusiveness and ubiquity, he had
carved out an artistic credo for himself early in his
career, as he explained: "If you want to know all about
Andy Warhol, just look at the surface of my paintings
and films and me, and there I am. There's nothing
behind it."[†] In his series of late self-portraits he pic-
tured himself in the role of the superstar, a concept he
singularly defined for late twentieth-century Americans.

This self-portrait, realized months before the artist's
sudden death, has assumed a peculiarly elegiac quality, reinforced by Warhol's ambiguous gaze, his
strangely detached head, and the frozen ballet of his
strawlike white wig. In the 1980s Warhol often paired
photographic, representational images with painterly,
abstract patterns, the strategy used for *Camouflage
Self-Portrait*. It was made by combining at least two
silk-screened images: one enlarged from a Polaroid
self-portrait, the second an abstract camouflage
pattern, which he translated from the typical military
olive drab into hot pink and red. Warhol's adoption of
camouflage, a mechanism for concealing identity,
could not be a better self-representation for an artist
who reproduced his own image repeatedly yet
remained ever the voyeur who kept his private self
far from the limelight.

KATE JAVENS (American, born 1959)

Named for Andrew Furuseth, 1996
Oil on theater muslin, 60 x 80 inches
Purchased with the Julius Bloch Memorial Fund

Named for Andrew Furuseth belongs to a group of animal paintings that Javens dedicated to obscure historical figures, defined as a group by their exceptional humanitarian activism or concern for social justice. A powerful photograph of Furuseth by Depression-era photographer Dorothea Lange attracted Javens when it was exhibited at the Philadelphia Museum of Art in 1994–95. Lange's image

of his weathered profile remained etched in Javens's memory when she made this meticulous painting of a crow to which she attached Furuseth's name. This humble yet magnificent creature becomes a portrait surrogate for Furuseth, who was known for his work as a founder of the Sailors' Union of the Pacific, an organization devoted to the welfare of seamen throughout the world. The relationship between the painted image and its title questions the nature of public identity and anonymity, producing an appropriate homage to modest, overlooked heroism.

Javens's approach to the rendering of the bird, which she found dead and brought to her studio to observe

and paint, engages with the American traditions of naturalism and realism. Early photography is purposefully recalled by the painting's sepia brown tonalities. In contrast to the contemporary obsession with celebrities and fame, Javens identified her decision to name the crow after Furuseth as part of a larger project of "reversing the process by which history forgets admirable, altruistic people."[†] Javens thinks of this as a kind of "tagging" that brings an unknown individual to public notice. Her painting lends immortality to a person and a creature whose deaths came together in the artist's imagination and studio.

NEIL JENNEY (American, born 1945)

Meltdown Morning, 1975
Oil on panel, 25¾ x 112½ inches
Gift (by exchange) of Samuel S. White 3rd and
Vera White, with additional funds contributed by
the Daniel W. Dietrich Foundation in honor of
Mrs. H. Gates Lloyd

A committed environmentalist, Jenney uses such real-life issues as acid rain and nuclear fallout as a springboard for aesthetic meditations on the North American landscape in the late twentieth century. The apocalyptic *Meltdown Morning* conveyed a cautionary message some four years before the accident at the Three Mile Island power plant awakened the American public to the chilling possibility of a nuclear disaster. The artist captured the cataclysmic horror of the atom bomb by focusing attention on the solitary tree trunk in the foreground. The massive tree looms so close to the picture plane that it obscures more than a third of the panel, forcing us to look around it, where in the far distance we see the ominous mushroom cloud and white light of a nuclear explosion. The calm beauty of this scene reveals Jenney's debt to nineteenth-century American landscape painters, especially the Hudson River School, whose picturesque Edens reflect the optimism of the American dream of Manifest Destiny. The artist's meticulous verisimilitude highlights the serene grandeur of the natural world at the very moment it faces catastrophic destruction. A thick black frame and sharply focused lighting enhance the painting's powerful sense of drama and mystery.

ANSELM KIEFER (German, born 1945)

Nigredo, 1984
Oil, acrylic, emulsion, shellac, and straw on
photograph and woodcut, mounted on canvas,
130 x 218½ inches
Gift of the Friends of the Philadelphia Museum of
Art in celebration of their 20th anniversary

Kiefer began *Nigredo* by covering nearly the entire
surface of a colossal canvas with a full-size photograph of a landscape. This photographic base was
then hidden by successive applications of thick layers
of viscous pigment, acrylic, emulsion, shellac, and
straw, producing a dense impasto with a charred
surface matching that of the apocalyptic wasteland

depicted in the painting. According to the artist, the
landscape was inspired by the sight of a field of peat
moss in Ireland, but there can be no mistaking the
underlying reference to World War II, the devastation
of Europe, and the destruction of German civilization
under the Nazi regime. The somber field of burnt
stubble can be read as an allegory of loss expressing
a collective yearning for pre-Nazi history, memories,
and countryside before Germany was bombed, burned,
and ravaged.

The artist represents the recent past as a furrowed
field rendered vast by the high horizon. Black boul-
ders, made using the traditional German medium of
the woodcut, occupy the foreground. Kiefer draws the
viewer into this deep, receding space with a series of

perspective lines leading to a single point on the horizon. The scrawled inscription "Nigredo" in the upper
left-hand corner of the painting refers to alchemy, the
medieval science that sought to transmute earth into
gold through a process of burning. Nigredo represents
the first stage of alchemical transformation, characterized by a black liquid, which is followed by the emer-
gence of a glowing light. The alchemists believed that
the creation of gold out of base matter was symbolic
of a far larger achievement, that of universal redemp-
tion. The faint gold behind the word Nigredo may refer
to the possibilities of spiritual and cultural renewal
in Germany after the cataclysmic horrors of the
twentieth century.

JOSEPH BEUYS (German, 1921–1986)

Lightning with Stag in Its Glare, 1987
Bronze, aluminum, and iron, height 20 feet
Gift (by exchange) of Bernard Davis, the estate of
Anna Goldthwaite, Mr. and Mrs. R. Sturgis Ingersoll,
James N. Rosenberg, the Chester Dale Gift, and
bequest of Lisa Norris Elkins

Lightning with Stag in Its Glare presents an eerie,
awesome vision of a silent world devoid of human
beings. Like most of Beuys's work, this installation
originated in the context of a specific occasion, in this
case an exhibition entitled "Zeitgeist," held in Berlin in
1982. Initially entitled "Workshop," the multipart installation centered on a towering mound of clay. Acknowl-
edging the temporary nature of his art, Beuys had
often preserved inevitably decaying organic materials
from such an installation in glass vitrines or recorded
the work in photographs. But in Berlin he decided to
create a permanent monument by casting the sculptures in metals; this casting was finished posthu-
mously.

In the 1960s Beuys had transformed the landscape
of German art with his provocative performances,
mysterious sculptures of fat and felt, and radical politics. His credo "everyone is an artist" embodied his
democratic all-inclusive view of creativity. At the same
time, his own autobiography formed an essential part
of his art. Several of the elements in this ensemble
reconstitute decades-old objects from his studio, and
re-create symbols that course through a lifetime of his
art. The enormous bolt of lightning embodies the electricity that was a powerful metaphor for creative
energy throughout Beuys's work, while the stag (here
cast from an old ironing board) long served as an alter
ego of the artist.

This ensemble presents a mythic landscape, mute
where it should be noisy, heavy where it should be
weightless, dark where it should be bright, inert where
it should be breathing. Whereas the initial "Workshop"
gave the feeling of an exploratory work-in-progress,
Lightning with Stag in Its Glare seems hauntingly final.

MARTIN PURYEAR (American, born 1941)

Old Mole, 1985
Red cedar, height 61 inches
Purchased with gifts (by exchange) of Samuel S.
White 3rd and Vera White, and Mr. and Mrs.
Charles C. G. Chaplin, and with funds contributed by
Marion Boulton Stroud, Mr. and Mrs. Robert Kardon,
Gisela and Dennis Alter, and Mrs. H. Gates Lloyd

Old Mole is a telling example of Puryear's ability to
meld modernist sculpture and craft traditions. This
simple, delicately handwrought, natural wood structure
embraces a vocabulary of materials and a formal
tradition that encompasses the elegant work of
Constantin Brancusi as well as the monumental
volumes and serial procedures that preoccupied many
artists in the 1970s. Puryear created the sculpture by
bending and weaving hundreds of slim wooden slats to
form a hollow volume, using a technique that recalls
boat-building or basketry. What initially looks like an
extremely systematic process is revealed to be the
result of unpredictable alternation of weft and warp,
mapped out partly with pencil lines. Pairs of tiny holes
remaining in many of the slats, left when temporary
staples were removed, suggest but do not fully divulge
the artist's manipulation of the organic materials used
to make the sculpture. The slats are permanently
affixed with short copper nails.

The sculpture rises from a large oval on the floor and
recedes from this broad base to a narrow, pointed
nose, nearly disappearing into space. Transforming
simple materials and geometry, the artist has crafted
a surprisingly talismanic object. In silhouette the sculpture looks like a beaked bird and from the back, like
an arching half-wheel. Charismatic and theatrical,
Old Mole is a reassuringly human-scaled object that
animates the viewer's space with its subtly confron-
tational presence.

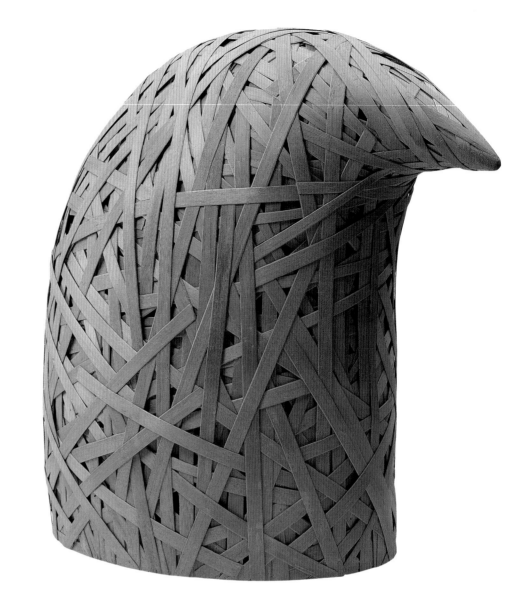

CHUCK CLOSE (American, born 1940)

Paul, 1994
Oil on canvas, 102 x 84 inches
Purchased with funds (by exchange) from the gift of
Mr. and Mrs. Cummins Catherwood, the Edith H. Bell
Fund, and with funds contributed by the Committee
on Twentieth-Century Art

The mammoth heads that Chuck Close painted almost
exclusively over the last three decades at the end of
the twentieth century reinvented portraiture. He works
from Polaroid photographs of faces, predominantly
stark black-and-white close-ups of fellow artists and
family that he takes himself. Then Close carefully covers them with a grid pattern and transposes the
images unit by unit onto canvases of monumental
size. This has been Close's working method since the
1960s, when he began painting in an exacting photo-
realist manner. His more recent paintings, in which he
has enlarged the scale of the grids and employed a
broader brush and richer colors, dramatize the tension
between the pure materiality of paint and its power of
illusionistic description. The free, lush passages of
pigment hover on the edge of abstraction and form a
legible portrait only when seen from a distance.

The subject of this iconic full-face portrait is the
esteemed American figurative artist Paul Cadmus,
who was ninety at the time of this painting and a
charismatic presence on the New York art scene for
more than half a century. When seen at close range,
the loosely handled paint surface dissolves into a
buoyant sea of blobs, resembling anything from
teardrops and doughnuts to the pixels that make up
digital imagery. Occasionally these shapes break out
of their designated grids, which are arranged diago-
nally in a diamond-patterned network, leading to further dissolution of the image. When the viewer slowly
backs away from the painting, the glimmering surface
gradually coalesces into a cohesive visage. Out of the
blur of mosaic-like color, one can begin to recognize
the distinctive ponytail, green eyes, and purple cravat
of this artist with whom Close shared a great mutual
admiration and affection.

GILBERT (English, born Italy, 1943) and
GEORGE (English, born 1942)

Red Morning Drowned, 1977
Gelatin silver prints, 23½ x 19¾ inches
Purchased with the Margaretta S. Hinchman
Fund, the Edgar Viguers Seeler Fund, the
Gertrud A. White Fund, and restricted matching
funds for contemporary acquisitions

Gilbert and George, who have been collaborating since
1967, have described their "Red Morning" series as
"a photographic painting of modern life."[†] The series
consists of seventeen multipaneled photo-pieces,
which share an interest in urban scenery such as high-
rise architecture, tree branches, and wet pavements,
some tinted a deep red, the color of darkroom light.
The artists have used the color red extensively in
their work, drawing on its symbolic associations with
blood, love, hate, and roses. It is also the national
color of China and the former Soviet Union. The subti-
tles of the "Red Morning" series reflect a deep anxiety
about the political situation in Britain in the late 1970s.
Such words as "Hell," "Violence," "Attack," "Killing,"
"Trouble," "Murder," and "Drowned" convey the sense
of impending disaster the artists felt at this time. The
photographs of the artists clad in white shirt sleeves,
without their trademark tweed suit jackets, somehow
mark them as particularly vulnerable.

Red Morning Drowned takes its title from the photographs of puddles that radiate out from the central
image of an office building facade, forming a cross.
These pools of water on the street carry reflections of
the sky and the surrounding environment. Like all the
images in this series, these photographs were taken in
the Spitalfields area of East London, a working-class
neighborhood where the artists live. The spire of
Nicholas Hawksmoor's Christ Church in Spitalfields, a
magnificent example of late Baroque architecture, is
reflected upside down in some of the puddles; this
landmark would be instantly recognizable to a British
audience. "Red Morning" is notable as the first series
in which the artists established the mural-sized grid
format that has remained standard for their photo-
pieces ever since.

RICHARD HAMILTON (English, born 1922)

Attic, 1995
Computer-printed transparencies on canvas,
48 x 96 inches
Purchased with funds contributed by the Committee
on Twentieth-Century Art, with additional funds
contributed by Mr. and Mrs. Keith L. Sachs, the
Dietrich Foundation, and Marion Boulton Stroud

In his computer-generated painting *Attic,* Hamilton
employed state-of-the-art technology to create a new
form of collage, replacing the old scissors-and-paste
method with the Quantel Paintbox, which is used by
television stations to produce computer graphics.
The Paintbox allows the artist to word-process with
images scanned into a Macintosh computer, in this
case using color transparencies of the top floor of
Hamilton's house and black-and-white photographs
of the Anthony d'Offay Gallery in London, where his
work is shown. The artist conflates domestic and
commercial spaces in the electronically manipulated
painting by "hanging" the image of his attic on the
simulated gallery wall so that the painting could be
seen to represent the space it inhabited.

Attic brings together many of the themes and images
that have preoccupied Hamilton over the course of his
long career. The black-and-white painting hanging on
the wall to the left is a work of 1966 entitled *People.*
The subject is an enlarged detail from a picture post-
card of a heavily populated beach at Whitley Bay, a
seaside town in the north of England. Below this picture, placed on the floor, is a study known as *Sieves*
that the artist made in 1965 while working on a
reconstruction of Marcel Duchamp's *Large Glass.*
Hamilton shares Duchamp's ironic, cerebral outlook
and is an authority on his work, having organized the
artist's retrospective exhibition at London's Tate Gallery in 1966. The only human presence in the otherwise unpopulated room appears in the form of Lord
Snowdon's photograph, seen on the far right, of the
German artist Joseph Beuys, who had been a friend
and collaborator of Hamilton's. Finally, the vacuum
cleaner that "hugs the rug closer here" continues the
artist's interest in the erotic overtones of domestic
appliances and advertising while also alluding in a
characteristically witty way to the obsessive neatness
of Hamilton's living space.

FELIX GONZALEZ-TORRES (American, born Cuba, 1957–1996)

Untitled (Petit Palais), 1992
Lightbulbs, electrical wire, and porcelain sockets,
length 62 feet
Gift of the Peter Norton Family Foundation

The modesty and open-ended quality of Felix Gonzalez-Torres's work have set the tone and direction of much significant art created in the 1990s. Like other examples of the work he created during his tragically short life, *Untitled (Petit Palais)* rejects a monumental and heroic tone in favor of a quietly personal approach. The artist identified his inspiration for this series as the delicate, decorative strands of light that graced an ordinary street fair in Paris. He inaugurated the light strands in 1991, the year that his companion died of AIDS. This example, comprised of forty-two frosted lightbulbs distributed on a 62-foot cord, is one of a group of twenty-four light strings that differ from one another in the titles given them by the artist and in the number and wattage of the bulbs themselves. Each sculpture can be arranged in any way a particular installer wishes, and thus holds the potential for unlimited variations.

Gonzalez-Torres's persistent ambition to link private or sociocultural associations to neutral objects was a subcurrent throughout his career. *Untitled (Petit Palais)* is therefore designed to admit a wide range of meanings, incorporating both the artist's and the viewer's responses and memories as well as the poignant tension between the capacity of light for revelation, purity, and transcendence and its inevitable dimming over time. Although the simplicity, anonymity, and serial nature of the light strands recall the formal structures and procedures of Minimalism, they are distinguished from that movement by their deeply expressive resonance.

GLENN LIGON (American, born 1960)

Untitled (I'm Turning Into a Specter Before Your Very Eyes and I'm Going to Haunt You), 1992
Oil and gesso on canvas, 80 x 30 inches
Purchased with the Adele Haas Turner and Beatrice
Pastorius Turner Memorial Fund

A painting fashioned from stenciled letters made in oil stick on canvas, Ligon's *Untitled (I'm Turning Into a Specter Before Your Very Eyes and I'm Going to Haunt You)* takes its place within the tradition of using language to make art and to question the meaning of representation. Like many painters and photographers of the 1980s and 1990s, Ligon became intrigued by research into the way culture and language shape identity. This painting belongs to a group of works he made in the early 1990s using words in black on white canvases and usually excerpting texts from literature by African American writers such as James Baldwin, Zora Neale Hurston, and Ralph Ellison. The source for *Untitled (I'm Turning Into a Specter Before Your Very Eyes and I'm Going to Haunt You)* is a 1959 play, *The Blacks (Les Nègres),* by the French writer Jean Genêt.

The artist made a slight but crucial alteration to Genêt's original text, transforming the original third-person voice into the first person. In Genêt's play, actors hide their identities by wearing black or white masks, an effect similar to Ligon's use of a borrowed quotation to distance the words from his own voice. His use of a stencil plate to form the letters suppresses the personality of his handwriting. Inspiring in the viewer a sense of curiosity about the identity of the speaker, Ligon's method also subtly suggests the complexities involved in representing racial identity in either paint or words. The transcribed text moves down the canvas with relentless, obsessive repetition, its legibility diminishing with the build-up of paint. As the lines of clearly visible words become more blurred and spectral, the marks emphasize the physical presence of the work as a painting while substantiating the content of the text itself.

KATHARINA FRITSCH (German, born 1956)

Knot, 1993
Plaster, iron, and pigment, 54 x 54 inches
Gift (by exchange) of Mr. and Mrs. R. Sturgis Ingersoll

Katharina Fritsch divides her work into what she half-jokingly calls "good" and "bad" pieces. She refers not to their quality but to the prevailing forces of innocence or darkness. *Knot* certainly belongs to the latter category, not only because of its jet-black color but because of the intense starkness that emanates from the perfection of its densely compact form. The formal beauty of Fritsch's archetypal knot—in use since ancient times—seems at odds with its invisible power: the sense is less that of a skillful sailor's knot than that of a "knotted" stomach or a handkerchief knotted in the sweaty hands of a person anxiously awaiting bad news. Fritsch's training at the Düsseldorf Academy in the late 1970s led her and her fellow students to an artistic style of clarity and exactitude. Particular to Fritsch is the disturbing vision to which she applies the neutral elements of symmetry, precision, and scale.

Close inspection of the sculpture's surface, which is composed of easily marred black matte pigment, reveals incised horizontal ridges that line the swelling strands of the knot. The ridges hint at the original identity of the piece: a knot that is formed by a tangle of long rat tails, a nightmarish phenomenon known in northern European folklore as the Rat-King. As the rats enmeshed in a Rat-King struggle and pull away to escape, they only tighten the knot that spells communal death. This sculpture was created as part of the Rat-King that Fritsch made for the Dia Center for the Arts in New York in 1993, an installation of sixteen 9-foot-tall black rats facing outward in a circle, almost hiding the knot at the center. Fritsch later excerpted the knot as an independent sculpture. Standing alone in a space it commands with uncanny authority, *Knot* is newly and richly open, although its elegant form remains freighted with the eeriness of its beginnings.

SIGMAR POLKE (German, born 1941)

Ginkgo, 1989
Gold, graphite, natural pigments, and synthetic resin
on woven polyester, 102 x 160 inches
Gift of the Friends of the Philadelphia Museum of Art

The shimmering surface of Sigmar Polke's *Ginkgo* is
both splendid and mysterious, a sensuous whirl of
silver, gold, cobalt, violet, and amber. The colors form
in great pools and swishes, pouring over and across
the surface in independent campaigns. The pigments
infuse multiple layers of resin and lacquer, which
together build up the glassy plane that confronts the
viewer. Two long panels of woven polyester provide
a translucent base on which these layers assume
their strangely ambiguous depths.

Polke insists on the experimental quality of his paintings of the late 1980s, which explore the nature of
pigments, minerals, dyes, and chemicals to the
degree that they might be characterized as two-
dimensional laboratories for the artist. *Ginkgo* is
distinguished by its suffusion of fields of small, slightly
raised dots, an effect caused by the drying process of
the transparent layers of resin. The dots effectively
destabilize the surface, which already appears to be
the site of accidents and random coincidences. The
long, feathery fissure in the lower right, for example,
at first alarmingly appears as if it were damaged; only
at close range does one see that it is safely lacquered
in place.

The idea of flux as an essential metaphor within all
of Polke's work is communicated by the title of the
painting, chosen after the completion of the work.
A Chinese word meaning "silver apricot," *Ginkgo*
names the tree with fan-shaped leaves that turn
golden yellow in autumn.

ZOE LEONARD (American, born 1961)

Strange Fruit (for David), 1992–97
Orange, banana, grapefruit, lemon, and avocado peels
with thread, zippers, buttons, sinew, needles, plastic,
wire, stickers, fabric, and trim wax, dimensions vary
with installation
Purchased with funds contributed by the Dietrich
Foundation and with the partial gift of the artist and
the Paula Cooper Gallery

Strange Fruit (for David) was made over the course
of five years from the rinds and skin of about three
hundred pieces of fruit that the artist and her friends
had eaten and then allowed to dry. She "repaired"
and adorned the opened seams with colored thread,

shiny wires, buttons, and zippers. Leonard explains
that the piece developed as a work of mourning after
a friend's death, "a sort of a way to sew myself back
up."[†] She began with two oranges sewn in Province-
town and continued in New York and later in Alaska,
where she relied on fruit sent to her by mail.

The quiet, elegiac tone of this piece contrasts with
Leonard's work from the late 1980s, when it was
inseparable from her activism on behalf of feminism,
gay rights, and the battle against AIDS. A powerful
body of impassioned, polemical, and sometimes crudely
made art had sprung from the anger and heartbreak
of a community ravaged by disease and death. To
Leonard, the experience of sewing the fruit seemed
to offer the reconciliation of beauty with her stance of

political engagement. Installed in the gallery, *Strange
Fruit* has the aura of a graveyard, a gathering of
strangers wherein each remains uniquely individual-
ized, a place hospitable to reverie and solace.

For as long as it lasts, the presence of the piece in
the Museum provides a powerful contemporary example of the venerable tradition of *vanitas* paintings,
meditations on the transience of life that usually portray fruit ready to decay, candles soon to gutter out,
or flowers about to fade. *Strange Fruit* removes art
from the fiction of a heroic "forever" and brings us
closer to human experience where everything is
changing or dying in some way but where beauty and
creativity still flourish.

PETER DOIG (British, born 1959)

Figure in Mountain Landscape II, 1998–99
Oil on canvas, 90¼ x 141¼ inches
Purchased with funds contributed by the Committee
on Twentieth-Century Art

Doig's painting adopts the grand scale of Abstract
Expressionist paintings by Jackson Pollock or Barnett
Newman but does so while addressing a traditional
narrative theme of a painter at work in a landscape.
Moveover, this painting's heroic size belies the fact
that it is based on a small black-and-white photograph:
an image of the Canadian artist Franklin Carmichael
sketching at Grace Lake in La Cloche Hills in

the 1930s. Carmichael was a member of the Group of
Seven, the best-known Canadian artists in the early
part of the twentieth century. Doig saw the photograph in the mid-1990s in the archives of the
McMichael Museum in Ottawa, a museum devoted to
the Group of Seven. He found himself powerfully drawn
to the image of the lone figure with his face hidden.
He photographed it through the glass display case and
returned to his studio in London to embark on what
would become a series of drawings and paintings that
use the image as a point of departure.

The familiarity of this painting's theme, often explored
in nineteenth-century art, is offset by the unusual nature
of its color and texture. Although painted in oils, the

surface seems closer to the transparent filminess of
watercolor, as seen especially in the lower foreground
grasses and reeds. The figure's painting-in-progress,
rendered in thick paint blobs in bubble-gum colors,
encourages the viewer to approach the canvas closely
but bears only the faintest resemblance to the
painter's surroundings. The hooded figure provides the
sole element of the painting that is green, the color of
landscape; the painter almost seems to be transforming into the landscape he paints. Doig leaves the
viewer in pleasurable uncertainty as to the layers of
fiction in the scene before him.

FRANZ WEST (Austrian, born 1947)

Delivery, 1997
Papier-mâché, gauze, plaster, paint, and wood, largest
unit, with base, 73⅛ x 28 x 23⅝ inches
Purchased with funds contributed by the Committee
on Twentieth-Century Art

The name of this work suggests the good-natured
spirit that Franz West has brought to the contemporary art world. Long promised as the centerpiece of
an exhibition opening in Portugal, it arrived at the very
last moment, bearing this modest but cheerfully triumphant title. The five-part sculpture incorporates works
West had made in the past as well as completely new

components. The pink element, for example, was new;
the tall yellow element was an older piece the artist
modified with a wrapping of yellow duct tape; and the
rabbit-shaped unit dates from a decade earlier.

West came of age during the heyday of the Vienna
Aktionists, a group of physically aggressive, often
violent performance artists in his native city. West
disliked the Aktionists' gory sensationalism, but he
was imbued with the sense of art as something to be
engaged with the body, actively produced and experienced. He called his first sculptural objects, made
in the mid-1970s, *passtücke,* or in an approximate
translation, "adaptives." The *passtücke* had no
pedestals and were meant to be moved around freely

by the viewer. By the mid-1980s, West also made
sculptures that are not participatory but retain the
bulbous informality, seemingly accidental surfaces,
and friendly scale of the *passtücke.*

Displayed on narrow pedestals, the components of
Delivery persuasively take their place in the family of
sculpture, whether Roman portrait busts or the
slender figures of Alberto Giacometti. But at the same
time they are willfully and merrily different in their
humble misshapenness and kindergarten colors, implic-
itly declaring that art can meet people at an ordinary
level, not as something sublime and sacred.

GABRIEL OROZCO (Mexican, born 1962)

Black Kites, 1997
Human skull and graphite, 8½ x 5 x 6½ inches
Gift (by exchange) of Mr. and Mrs. James P. Magill

Orozco's *Black Kites,* in the artist's own description, is a drawing in three dimensions. A bleached human skull traversed by a lead pencil design, the sculpture provocatively integrates structure and surface, line and volume. Like that of many artists of his generation, Orozco's aesthetic favors modest over monumental and reveals unexpected sensuality in common objects and materials. Although in *Black*

Kites Orozco took up a motif deeply entrenched in the popular art and tradition of his native Mexico, he transformed it into a strikingly contemporary object of rich ambiguity.

The sculpture's checkered design is far more complicated than it first appears. The pattern originated in a labyrinthine set of lines that the artist drew in graphite over the entire surface of the skull, including even the eye sockets. The imposition of a flat gridlike design on a naturally irregular shape inevitably required strategic compression and elongation, with dramatic twists and turns. Orozco titled a photograph of the work in progress *Paths of*

Thought, hinting that the black patterning expressed the fluidity and complexity of a living brain within a rigid skull. It evokes the paradox of cognitive thought, with all its implications of order and system, as part of an organic, imperfect being.

The work's title is typical of Orozco's allusive names for his sculptures, installations, photographs, and drawings. The mental image of black diamond-shaped kites floating through the sky transports the heavy, earthbound skull into an airborne poem. At the turn of a new century, Orozco reinvokes the romantic vision of art's power to send man soaring beyond his earthly limits.

Notes

Page 24

W. Warshawsky, "Orpheism, Latest of Painting Cults," *The New York Times,* October 19, 1913, p. 4; quoted in *František Kupka, 1871–1957: A Retrospective* (New York: The Solomon R. Guggenheim Foundation, 1975), p. 31.

Page 27

American Art News, vol. 11, no. 21 (March 1, 1913), p. 3, and vol. 11, no. 22 (March 8, 1913), p. 3.

Page 32

Quoted in *Alexander Archipenko: A Centennial Tribute,* by Katherine Jánszky Michaelsen and Nehama Guralnik (Washington, D.C.: National Gallery of Art, 1986), p. 39.

Page 38

John Sloan's New York Scene, from the Diaries, Notes, and Correspondence, 1906–1913, edited by Bruce St. John (New York: Harper & Row, 1965), pp. 308–9.

Page 39

Louis Michel Eilshemius, *The Art Reformer,* vol. 2 (September–December 1911), p. 8.

Page 41

Pierre Bonnard's notes, February 1, 1934, Bibliothèque Nationale, Paris; quoted in *Bonnard: The Late Paintings,* by John Russell (New York and London: Thames & Hudson, 1984), p. 69.

Page 51

Arthur Jerome Eddy, *Cubists and Post-Impressionism* (Chicago: A. C. McClurg, 1914), p. 128.

Page 58

Jean Guichard-Meili, *Matisse,* translated by Caroline Moorehead (New York: Praeger, 1967), p. 168.

Page 59

Theodore Reff, "Picasso's Three Musicians: Maskers, Artists & Friends," *Art in America,* vol. 68, no. 10 (December 1980), pp. 124–42.

Page 60

Kurt Schwitters, "Die Merzmalerei," *Der Sturm,* vol. 10, no. 4 (July 1919), p. 61; quoted in *Kurt Schwitters,* by John Elderfield (London: Thames & Hudson, 1985), p. 50.

Page 62

Marcel Duchamp, *Marcel Duchamp, Criticavit*; quoted in *Salt Seller: The Writings of Marcel Duchamp (Marchand du sel),* edited by Michel Sanouillet and Elmer Peterson (New York: Oxford University Press, 1973), p. 144.

Page 68

Joaquín Torres-García, "Vouloir construire," *Cercle et Carré,* no. 1 (March 15, 1930), n.p.; quoted in *The Planar Dimension: Europe, 1912–1932,* by Margit Rowell (New York: The Solomon R. Guggenheim Foundation, 1979), p. 96.

Page 70

James Ensor, in "Discours au Kursaal d'Ostende," *Mes écrits,* translated by Caroline Beamish (Liège: Ed. Nationales, 1974), p. 143; quoted in *James Ensor, 1860–1969: Theatre of Masks,* edited by Carol Brown (London: Lund Humphries, 1997), p. 12.

Page 72

Undated letter from Horace Pippin, Horace Pippin War Memoirs, Letters, and Photographs, Archives of American Art, Smithsonian Institution, Washington, D.C.; quoted in *I Tell My Heart: The Art of Horace Pippin,* by Judith E. Stein (Philadelphia: Pennsylvania Academy of the Fine Arts, 1993), p. 3.

Page 76

Salvador Dali, *The Secret Life of Salvador Dali,* translated by Haakon M. Chevalier (New York: Dial Press, 1942), p. 357.

Page 77

Translated in *Man Ray: American Artist,* by Neil Baldwin (New York: Clarkson N. Potter, 1988), p. 207.

Page 80

Sidney Janis, *Abstract and Surrealist Art in America* (New York: Reynal & Hitchcock, 1944), p. 112.

Page 86
Quoted in *Alice Trumbull Mason, Emily Mason: Two Generations of Abstract Painting,* by Marilyn Brown (New York: Eaton House, 1982), p. 20.

Page 87
Quoted in *Stuart Davis,* edited by Diane Kelder (New York: Praeger, 1971), p. 104.

Page 90
John Bartlow Martin, with drawings by Ben Shahn, "The Blast in Centralia No. 5: A Mine Disaster No One Stopped," *Harper's Magazine,* vol. 196, no. 1174 (March 1948), pp. 193–220.

Page 91
"Phila. Museum Pays $35,000 for Canvas by Penna. Artist Wyeth," *The Philadelphia Inquirer,* September 30, 1959, p. 16.

Page 104
Gene Baro, "Some Late Words from David Smith," *Art International,* vol. 9, no. 7 (October 20, 1965), p. 49.

Page 107
Quoted in *Duchamp: A Biography,* by Calvin Tomkins (New York: Henry Holt, 1996), p. 451.

Page 111
Interview with Walter Hopps, *Artforum,* March 1965; reprinted in *Jasper Johns: Writings, Sketchbook Notes, Interviews,* edited by Kirk Varnedoe (New York: The Museum of Modern Art, 1996), p. 113.

Page 112
Agnes Martin, *Writings: Schriften,* edited by Dieter Schwarz (Stuttgart: Cantz Verlag, 1991), p. 153.

Page 114
Quoted in *Catalogue of The Tate Gallery's Collection of Modern Art,* by Ronald Alley (London: The Tate Gallery, 1981), p. 81.

Page 123
Sam Hunter and Don Hawthorne, *George Segal* (New York: Rizzoli, 1984), p. 35.

Page 134
Quoted in Deborah Solomon, "Celebrating Paint," *The New York Times Magazine,* March 31, 1991, p. 40.

Page 136
Quoted in *Gerhard Richter: Paintings,* by Roald Nasgaard (London: Thames & Hudson, 1988), p. 77.

Page 137
Neue Nationalgalerie, Berlin, *Andy Warhol* (Berlin: Gerd Fleischmann, 1969), n.p.

Page 138
Author's interview with the artist, spring 1999, Philadelphia Museum of Art.

Page 144
Quoted in *Europe in the Seventies: Aspects of Recent Art,* by Jean-Christophe Ammann (Chicago: The Art Institute, 1977), p. 19.

Page 150
Interview with the artist by Anna Blume, January 18, 1997, Paula Cooper Gallery, New York.

Other titles of interest from the Philadelphia Museum of Art

The Louise and Walter Arensberg Collection: 20th Century Section, introduction by Henry Clifford, 1954

A. E. Gallatin Collection: "Museum of Living Art," introduction by A. E. Gallatin, 1954

Marcel Duchamp, by Anne d'Harnoncourt and Kynaston McShine, 1973

Raymond Duchamp-Villon: Pioneer of Modern Sculpture, by Judith Zilczer, *Philadelphia Museum of Art Bulletin,* Fall 1980

Walter Conrad Arensberg: Poet, Patron, and Participant in the New York Avant-Garde, 1915–20, by Francis Nauman, *Philadelphia Museum of Art Bulletin,* Spring 1980

Structured Subject in Contemporary Art: Reflections on Works in the Twentieth-Century Galleries, by Mark Rosenthal, *Philadelphia Museum of Art Bulletin,* Fall 1983

Manual of Instructions for Marcel Duchamp "Étant Donnés: 1 la chute d'eau, 2 le gaz d'éclairage," introduction by Anne d'Harnoncourt, 1987

Étant Donnés 1. La chute d'eau 2. Le gaz déclairage: Reflections on a New Work by Marcel Duchamp, by Anne d'Harnoncourt and Walter Hopps, *Philadelphia Museum of Art Bulletin,* 1987 (Second reprint of 1969 Bulletin)

Miró, by Ann Temkin, *Philadelphia Museum of Art Bulletin,* Fall 1987

The A. E. Gallatin Collection: An Early Adventure in Modern Art, by Gail Stavitsky, *Philadelphia Museum of Art Bulletin,* Winter 1994

Paintings from Europe and the Americas in the Philadelphia Museum of Art: A Concise Catalogue, 1994

African American Artists, by Glenn C. Tomlinson and Rolando Corpus, *Philadelphia Museum of Art Bulletin,* Winter 1995

Constantin Brancusi, by Friedrich Teja Bach, Margit Rowell, and Ann Temkin, 1995

Philadelphia Museum of Art: Handbook of the Collections, 1995

Mad for Modernism: Earl Horter and His Collection, by Innis Howe Shoemaker, with essays by Christa Clarke and William Wierzbowski, 1999

Index of Artists

Permissions